D1743758

City Breaks
in
Venice
– a new look

REG BUTLER

In Association with

THOMSON HOLIDAYS

SETTLE PRESS

Text © 1994 Reg Butler
Second Edition 1997

First published by Settle Press
10 Boyne Terrace Mews
London W11 3LR

ISBN (Paperback) 1 872876 52 8

Printed by Villiers Publications
19 Sylvan Avenue
London N3 2LE

Foreword

As Britain's leading short breaks specialist, we recognise the need for detailed information and guidance for City Break travellers. But much more is required than just a listing of museums and their opening times. For a few days, the City Break visitor wants to experience the local continental lifestyle.

Reg Butler has had considerable experience of the great Italian cities. As a young courier, he conducted ten full seasons of grand European tours, with regular visits to Venice, Florence and Rome. Since then he has returned many times to Italy, writing travel articles for British and American newspapers and magazines.

For this book, Reg Butler collaborated closely with our resident Thomson staff, who have year-round experience of helping visitors enjoy these cities. We're sure you'll find this book invaluable in planning how to make best personal use of your time.

In this revised edition, all opening hours, prices, phone numbers and restaurant recommendations have been checked by Thomson's resident office staff and reps in Venice. They have the huge advantage of being able to monitor changes as they happen. But, inevitably, more changes will occur between the date of printing and when the reader travels.

As well as City Breaks in Italy, other books in the series cover Paris, Amsterdam, Central Europe, Spain, New York, Dublin, Bruges and Brussels. Thomson also operate to many other world cities from departure points across the UK.

THOMSON CITYBREAKS

Contents

4

Chapter One

Introduction

1.1 City of Gondola Romance

Part of the fun of Venice is seeing first-hand how a city can work without wheels.

There's real theatre about your arrival, whether you come by the road or rail causeway across the Venetian lagoon, or by direct water transport from the airport.

Main Street is the Grand Canal: two miles long, eighty yards wide, and shaped like the backward 'S' of a simple speller. All is magnificence. The finest palaces, churches, museums and mansions line its banks. Every bend offers a vista that seems almost too highly-coloured to be true.

The essential monuments – Cathedral, Clock Tower, Campanile, Doges' Palace – stand side by side on St Mark's Square, where rival open-air café orchestras play for their clientele and anyone who happens to be strolling past.

That's an entertainment in itself, just sitting for an hour, enjoying a drink and idly watching the world-wide cross-section of brightly-dressed tourists and pretty girls. It all makes a romantic setting that has delighted visitors for several hundred years.

You pay a high price for the location – for the privilege of taking your refreshment in one of Europe's most beautiful squares, virtually unchanged since the 16th century. But few visitors complain at the bill, when the entire theatrical scene is so perfectly designed for leisure.

Go just around the corner to a side-canal bar, and a similar drink will cost barely one-third the price, but give only one-tenth that 'atmosphere'.

Random delight

There's great enjoyment in venturing through medieval alleys into a little piazza (locally called campo), walking beside canals and over the hump-backed bridges. Everywhere you point your camera, there are pictures. Just drift around at random, away from the main stream of tourism, and you'll find new delight at every corner.

Take a carefree attitude towards time, and getting lost for an hour doesn't matter. Distances are really quite small, as in Hampton Court Maze. An expert navigator can walk right across Venice in 30 minutes. The less expert could make out in two or three hours, but would carry away a lifetime's memory of a journey through the Middle Ages. That's the Venetian experience.

Some folk arrive in Venice with their noses twitching for a dubious-smelling canal. In the hotel, the first thing they do is to fling open their bedroom window and take a deep suspicious breath. In fact, it's true that – come July and August – there is ripeness in the air.

But full enjoyment of Venice depends how you approach it. Read up some potted history – the incredible story of how a group of muddy islands became the greatest art and trading centre of medieval Europe – and the Venice of today will really come alive.

It all started in 5th century AD, when the Roman Empire was falling apart and Barbarians were sweeping down the middle of Italy. A few refugees from mainland cities settled in these islands, protected by waters of the Lagoon. They stayed independent, and elected their first *dux* or Doge in year 726.

Over the centuries, the Venetians became shrewd traders and businessmen, linking the trading routes from Asia Minor to northern Europe. Commanding the main route to the Holy Land, they particularly made big profits from the Crusades – cash down, and a share of the loot for providing army transport ships. As part of the contracts, the Venetians acquired trading rights in many Levant cities, and supremacy in the Adriatic.

Riches of the past

Their biggest pay-off came from the Crusader sacking of Constantinople in 1204. Quite apart from their share of Byzantine treasures, the Venetians gained control of all strategic locations and trading posts in Eastern Mediterranean and through to the Black Sea. Venice commanded the Silk Route to the Far East, and had a virtual monopoly of the over-land spice trade from the Indies.

Thanks to that commercial supremacy, the merchants and ruling families of Venice became extremely wealthy. They lined the Grand Canal with rich palaces and public buildings, furnished with great luxury. Artists and craftsmen flocked to the city, where big money flowed.

Later, the power of Venice dwindled. The Turks captured Constantinople in 1453. With expansion of the Ottoman Empire, the Venetians lost most of their maritime possessions.

A major blow to their commercial supremacy came in 1486, when Vasco da Gama opened up a new round-the-Cape sea route for the spice trade. With discovery of the Americas, Venice was on the 'wrong' side of the Mediterranean to exploit the business potential.

In early 16th century, many Venetian territories were carved up by an alliance called the League of Cambrai, comprising the European powers, the Church, and other Italian States.

But, despite the trading decline and loss of em-pire, Venice still flourished as the aristocratic fun city of Europe, full of courtesans, festivals, masked balls, high-stake gambling, pleasure of every kind.

Venice was an essential staging-point on a wealthy young man's Grand Tour, whence he could return to his country estate with souvenir sculptures and paintings.

All the great Italian painters – Giorgione, Titian, Tintoretto, Veronese, and then Canaletto and many others – found a rich clientele for their work, and dozens of churches to decorate.

The good days continued until the French Revo-lution, followed by several decades of melancholy and neglect.

INTRODUCTION

Festivals and fun

For the past hundred-odd years, international tourism has kept Venice alive – just as international aid funds are helping to prevent Venice sinking permanently into the mud.

The festival tradition continues, and Venice keeps its reputation as one of the great fun cities of Europe. It's a wonderful place to enjoy yourself, with masses of culture as an excuse for going, if you need an excuse.

A visit to Venice is a journey into the past, greatly enlivened by the present. Few other cities have such magnificent antique stores, alternating with glass stores and workshops where the traditions of craftsmanship are totally unchanged from centuries ago.

Venice is an art-lovers' paradise, with many of the world's greatest paintings and sculptures. But its full appeal is not buried in museums. No other city on earth can rival that incredible architecture, preserved totally unchanged over the centuries. You can identify every building of the centre just by looking at reproductions of the paintings of Canaletto, who recorded the 18th-century Venetian cityscape in the finest detail.

Step carelessly off the pavement in any other Italian city, and you risk being mown down by passing traffic. It's quite different in Venice, where you can wander and gossip in the middle of the street, just like a thousand years ago when the original paving stones were laid.

Chapter Two
Arrival in Venice

2.1 When to go

Outside the April till October season, the glamour city of the Venetian Lagoon is sleepy, except for special events like Carnival (late February), when the 18th century is revived with masked balls and pageants.

Otherwise, many shops close throughout winter, and you may need Wellington boots to cross St Mark's Square.

Springtime, especially at Easter, the big rush starts, and Venice awakens to exuberant activity. Visitors by the thousand flock through the central piazza – trailing behind their guide-lecturers in the morning, free in the afternoon.

Night-time, the canals echo to the sound of Gondola Serenades.

In the hotter summer months, many sightseers adopt the good Italian tradition of an afternoon siesta. It's not a 'waste' of time.

You are then refreshed for a cooler return to the sightseeing circuits, followed by the tranquil pleasures of open-air dining, watching the world go by from pavement cafés or participating in a Gondola Serenade. In the evening there's more space to move around, after day-trip crowds from inland cities and neighbouring Adriatic resorts have returned to base.

Autumn is well worth considering, for easier progress around the tourist sites. Hotel tariffs become more reasonable, and shopkeepers heavily discount their goods or are open to offers rather than carry them unsold through the winter.

2.2 Arrival in Venice

How to reach your hotel, in a city without roads? For travellers on a City Break holiday, a tour-operator 'transfer' is normally included in the package. These folk can just relax, and let the local representative cope with all those boatmen, shouting and waving their arms in Venetian dialect.

But for a first-timer arriving in Venice without travel-agency help, the transport system can seem wildly confusing.

Keep calm! It's not really so chaotic. After centuries of playing host to vast numbers of foreign visitors, the Venetians are expert in moving people and baggage between arrival point and their hotel destination.

Venice is an archipelago of 118 islands with 150 canals and over 400 bridges. Only two of those islands can be reached from the mainland, except by boat.

Since 1846, Venice has been linked to the Italian transport system by a railway bridge; and, since 1933, by a two-mile causeway to the Piazzale Roma which faces the rail terminus just across the Grand Canal.

From those two access points, everything moves only on foot or on water.

Hotels are either north of the Rialto Bridge – that is, closer to Piazzale Roma or the Santa Lucia railway station (usually known as Ferrovia); or closer to the main monuments, south of Rialto Bridge, with San Marco as the focal point.

Arrival by air

Marco Polo Airport is on the mainland, to the east of industrial-city Mestre. Your target is either Piazzale Roma, or San Marco. Here are the choices:

By bus

The blue A.T.V.O. coach runs frequently from the Airport to Piazzale Roma, Venice. Tickets costing 5,000 lire are sold at the desk by the main exit in the arrivals hall. Journey time is 25 minutes.

There's also a local public bus (A.C.T.V.) which is orange, and costs only 1,500 lire. Tickets are available at the Airport Bar. But it's a long journey, stopping at every halt along the route. Not recommended!

By land taxi

From the Airport to Piazzale Roma costs about 50,000 lire including luggage, but agree the price before setting off. Journey time is 15 minutes.

By public water taxi to San Marco

The label is 'Motoscafo in Servizio Pubblico'. Buy your ticket costing 15,000 lire at the A.C.T.V. desk inside the airport building. Journey time is one hour.

By private water taxi

The cost direct to your hotel will probably be about 130,000 lire, but make sure of the price before departure.

Arrival by car or motor-coach

All bus and coach services bring you across the Lagoon to the terminal at Piazzale Roma.

By private car, you can likewise drive across to Piazzale Roma, where signs point to giant multi-storey garages or open-air parkings which charge high tariffs.

Better strategy is to park on the mainland – at Mestre, for instance – and do the last sector by coach or train.

Arrival by train

If you're looking after your own travel movements, you'll find the waterbus stop just outside.

(See the Public Transport section later in this chapter, for the stops served by the waterbuses.)

Porters

For the final stage to your hotel, you can either take a water taxi (expensive) or a gondola (costing much more); or use your own two feet, if only you can find which way to point them! A set of wheels for your suitcase can be very helpful.

If your suitcases are heavy, you can hire a porter to escort you to the hotel, and help you negotiate bridges. Be absolutely sure to establish the price before setting off. You'll be lucky to agree a price of 20,000 lire for one or two pieces of luggage!

Departure from Venice
On your departure, transport will seem so much simpler. For the airport, take the public water taxi direct from San Marco; or get to Piazzale Roma by waterbus and thence go by coach.

2.3 Your hotel

Most hotels in Venice are old-style properties. The keyword is 'old'. They all have lots of character.

Venice is a city which lives off the past. Virtually all buildings come under very strict preservation orders from the Town Council. For this reason, it's very difficult for any new works to be carried out. Some hotels have still not obtained permission even to display their own hotel sign outside the front door.

Other hoteliers applied years ago for a licence to instal a lift, and are still awaiting an answer. So don't expect a high-rise hotel which is all 20th-century concrete, glass and chromium plating. Frankly, it would be most disappointing, if that's what you found in Venice!

Check-in: Normal check-in and check-out time is midday, but confirm with reception. If you arrive before noon, you may check in and leave luggage with reception until your room is free.

If your final departure is after midday, pack bags before going out for the morning and leave them in the left-luggage room.

Getting in late: Some hotels lock their doors after midnight. If you plan to be out late, advise the concierge beforehand, just to be sure that a night porter can let you in!

Electricity: Plugs are generally Continental-style two-pin. Pack a plug adaptor if you expect to use your own electric gadgets. Electricity is mostly 220 volts. But some of the oldest hotels still use 110 volts, so check before using any equipment. If you need a transformer, ask your concierge.

Lighting: Hotel corridors sometimes have a time switch for the lights, which operate long enough to unlock your door. Look for a small orange light and press the button.

Water taps: 'C' stands for *caldo*, meaning hot; 'F' is *freddo*, meaning cold.

Breakfast: Italian breakfasts are modest Continental – bread or rolls, jam or marmalade, a helping of butter, and tea or coffee. Normally it's served early, available between 7.30 and 9.30. Cooked items are available at extra charge.

Tipping: Around 1,000 lire per case is usual for porters. Chambermaids will appreciate any lire you leave for them at the end of your stay.

2.4 Orientation and transport

After the first few hours, you'll start getting your bearings. Study a map, and check how your hotel relates to the main points of Venice.

The Grand Canal itself is the great Main Street of Venice, running in backward-S shape from the Railway Station and Piazzale Roma at the northwest end, through to St Mark's at the south.

Only three bridges cross the Grand Canal: Scalzi – north, by the Railway Station, linking the districts (*sestieri*) of Cannaregio and Santa Croce; Rialto – central, linking San Polo and Castello; Accademia – south, linking San Marco and Dorsoduro.

Once these focus points are fixed in your mind, Venice becomes much less confusing. Virtually all of the 118 islands of Venice has a church, usually with an adjoining *campo* or square which serves as a navigation point. Streets could better be described as passageways, wandering between the bridges among the tightly-packed buildings.

The great key to orientation is the Venetian way-marking system of black arrows on yellow signs that point to the pedestrian hubs of S. Marco, Rialto, Accademia, Ferrovia (railway station) and Piazzale Roma. The most densely used route zigzags from the Clock Tower at St Mark's Square to the Rialto. Lined with high-grade shops the whole way, the route is called the Merceria.

The public transport system is wrapped around key staging points along the waterways. The Venetian water buses – 'Vaporetti' (steamers, but now running on diesel) – are almost as famous as the gondolas, but not nearly so romantic.

Every waterbus stop is clearly marked with its name. Signs point the way from the landing-stage to the neighbouring points of tourist interest. Likewise, if you're lost in the maze, sooner or later you'll spot a sign to Vaporetti or to one of the Venetian focal points. Try it!

Ticketing

Vaporetti tickets are sold at the entrance to each water bus stand. But you can also buy tickets on board, at an 800-lire supplement. Standard single fares are 4,500 lire, and each suitcase is likewise charged 4,500 lire. Tickets must be cancelled in the time-dating machine before entering the landing stage area. Anyone caught aboard without a validated ticket risks an on-the-spot fine.

A tourist ticket ('Biglietto Turistico') costs 15,000 lire and is valid for 24 hours on any line; or 30,000 lire for 72 hours (time begins at the first journey, so that 72 hours can mean the best part of four days). A 7-day ticket costs 55,000 lire.

These long-term tickets are excellent value. Buy them on arrival, when yourself and suitcase will anyway cost 9,000 lire from the railway station or Piazzale Roma – and the same amount for the return (unless your hotel is within walking distance). It's very handy to be able to hop on and off water-buses throughout your stay, and will also save you queuing for tickets and time-stamping each time.

Vaporetti routes

The water buses run every ten minutes or so during the day, and less frequently after midnight.

There are 20 numbered bus stops on the main Canal Grande to Lido route:

1 – Piazzale Roma: for arrivals and departures by road across the causeway by car or bus.

2 – Ferrovia: for S. Lucia railway station; easy reach of Ghetto; Scalzi Bridge.

3 – Riva di Biagio: for Fondaco dei Turchi (Museum of Natural History).

4 – San Marcuola: for Ghetto and Cannaregio district.

5 – San Staè: for Modern Art Museum,

6 – Ca' d'Oro: for Franchetti Gallery.

7 – Rialto: for the Bridge; Rialto market; Merceria shopping route to St Mark's.

8 – San Silvestro: for Campo San Polo and district.

9 – San Angelo.

10 – San Tomà: for Frari Church; San Rocco.

11 – Ca' Rezzonico: for Palazzo Rezzonico (Museum of the Settecento).

12 – Accademia: for the Bridge; Accademia Gallery; Peggy Guggenheim Gallery.

13 – Santa Maria del Giglio: for Fenice Theatre square.

14 – Salute: for S. Maria della Salute; Dogana di Mare (Old Customs House); Peggy Guggenheim Gallery.

15 – San Marco: for the historic centre.

16 – San Zaccaria: for Church; historic centre.

17 – Arsenale: for Naval History Museum; Arsenal.

18 – Giardini (Esposizione): for public gardens.

19 – Santa Elena: for Remembrance Park.

20 – Lido: for summer beach, Casino and International Film Festival.

Route 1

Calls at every stop from 1 to 20. Stops 1 to 15 (San Marco) cover the entire length of the Grand Canal. Journey time, right through to Lido – one hour; or about 45 minutes to San Marco.

Beware of pickpockets on crowded transport.

CANNAREGIO

New Ghetto

Old *Ghetto*

T

Canal Grande

③

④

⑤

S

Q

R

U

Railway Station

②

SANTA CROCE

SAN POLO

San Polo

⑧

V

①

Piazzale
← Roma

M

⑩

⑨

SAN MAR

Canal Grande

L

⑪

⑫

⑬

J

K

DORSODURO

Maritime Terminal

Canale

della

Isla

VENICE

See the number keys on next page

A Principal sites

6 Water bus stops

N

T

5

P

N

7

O

W

CASTELLO

F B
A C D
E G

16

17

15

CO

Canale di San Marco

14
I

H

Giudecca

San Giorgio Maggiore

Canale San Giorgio

Giudecca

VENICE
- the key locations

K - Accademia Gallery
K - Accademia Bridge
X - Arsenal
D - Bridge of Sighs
Q - Ca' d'Oro
R - Ca' Pesaro
F - Clock Tower
C - Doge's Palace
D - Ducal Prison
S - Fondaco dei Turchi
Q - Franchetti Gallery
G - Giardinetti
T - Jewish Ghetto
R - Modern Art Museum
S - Museum of Natural History
R - Museum of Oriental Art

E - Museum of the Risorgimento
E - Museum of the Settecento
Y - Naval History Museum
L - Palazzo Rezzonico
J - Peggy Guggenheim Collection
A - Piazza San Marco
V - Piazzale Roma
Z - Public Gardens
N - Rialto Bridge
H - San Giorgio Maggiore
P - San Zanipolo
M - Santa Maria dei Frari
I - S. Maria della Salute
O - Santa Maria Formosa
U - Scalzi Bridge
M - Scuola Grande di San
        Rocco
W - Scuola di San Giorgio
        deglie Schiavoni
B - St Mark's Basilica
A - St Mark's Square

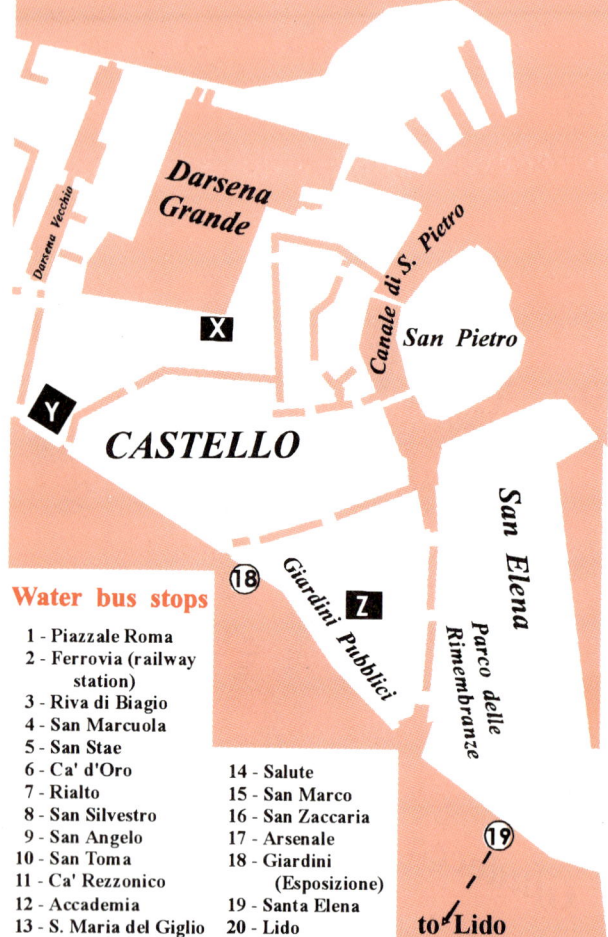

Water bus stops

1 - Piazzale Roma
2 - Ferrovia (railway
        station)
3 - Riva di Biagio
4 - San Marcuola
5 - San Stae
6 - Ca' d'Oro
7 - Rialto
8 - San Silvestro
9 - San Angelo
10 - San Toma
11 - Ca' Rezzonico
12 - Accademia
13 - S. Maria del Giglio

14 - Salute
15 - San Marco
16 - San Zaccaria
17 - Arsenale
18 - Giardini
        (Esposizione)
19 - Santa Elena
20 - Lido

Route 82
There are two types of this Express service with fewer stops: from Piazzale Roma (stop 1) via Grand Canal to St Mark's; and Grand Canal, Piazzale Roma, Tronchetto, Giudecca Canal and Lido (in summer only).

Route 52
A circle line, both ways, going round the perimeter of the main body of Venice, including Murano to the north, and S. Giorgio Maggiore and La Giudecca to the south. The full circuit takes 1 hour 45 minutes.

Water taxis
A luxurious way to travel. There are numerous taxi stands. Always settle the price before embarking. Reckon a starting price of 70,000 lire.

Traghetto
A gondola-type ferry from one side of the Grand Canal to the other. You ride it standing up, so be sure you have your 'sea legs'! Cost: 600 lire.

Gondolas
Gondola transport is picturesque but pricey. The gondoliers operate a scheduled tariff according to time or distance. Locals – and most tourists, once they've learnt the system – take the water-bus, which is far cheaper.

The problem is that the 500 remaining gondoliers of Venice can earn a living only during a tourist season of six months, but want to feed their families year-round. There's just no alternative employment during off season.

However, despite the cost, most visitors go at least once for a gondola ride – maybe as part of a daytime tour with great photo opportunities, or on a moonlight Gondola Serenade.

More expensive, try hiring one yourself – having agreed the price first – and sit back to enjoy a unique transport experience. The starting price is 80,000 lire for fifty minutes in daytime, or 100,000 lire after 8 p.m.

How to steer one-sided

By official decree dated 1562, gondoliers may paint their 33-ft boats any colour they like, so long as it's black. The design is traditional, with origins going back to the 7th century AD. A gondola weighs around 1500 lbs, and is deliberately skewed to counterbalance the tough problem of propelling and steering with only one oar.

Watch the steering. To stop his boat waltzing round and round, the gondolier uses a double stroke. The main drive comes from *pushing* on the oar. That sends the boat onwards, but swerving left. The return stroke is made under water, with blade almost flat. That swings the gondola to the right, rocking it gently. Progress is a mild series of zig-zags.

Despite the medieval setting, the 20th century still rears its head. Waterbuses and taxis are fitted with hooters. Speed cops patrol in launches to check motorboat drivers whose wash causes erosion.

General rule of the canal is Keep Left. That is logical enough, for the gondola's one oar is always on the right. But there's a special Waterway Code for cornering. Stationed at the rear of a 33-ft boat, gondoliers must naturally corner blind. Whoever shouts first can swing out and take a corner wide, passing left or right. It all works, quite smoothly, no bad language.

Chapter Three

Plan your sightseeing

3.1 The basic highlights

When John Ruskin wrote *The Stones of Venice*, he left not a stone uncovered. But the project of writing about virtually every significant building took him eight years to complete, from 1845 to 1853.

For the modern visitor with less time to spare, here's a short list of Essential Venice, aimed at capturing the flavour of this fantastic City Without Roads.

• Take the standard tour of St Mark's and the Doges' Palace.

• Linger with a coffee or beer at an outdoor café on St Mark's Square, and hang the expense but mind the pigeons.

• Duck through the Clock Tower archway into the Merceria, and follow that narrow, winding shopping street through to Rialto Bridge.

• Try to remember some of Shylock's lines, as you cross the Rialto Bridge into the heart of the bubbling market area – always a trading centre since before the days of Shakespeare's *Merchant of Venice*.

• See the Grand Canal by slow water bus – 45 minutes with 15 bus-stops for 4,500 lire. This journey is also top favourite for the jostle-and-pickpocket teams. Watch your purse or wallet, as well as the palaces!

• If you're desperate for a sandy-beach session, travel by waterbus across to the Lido where hotels charge steeply for access; or go to the free but scruffy public beaches at each end.

• Take a trip to the glass-manufacturing island of Murano, the lace-making of Burano, and to Torcello where the original Venice was established.

• Schedule a culture-vulture visit to the Galleria dell'Accademia for the world's finest collection of Venetian paintings from the 15th to 18th centuries.

• One beautiful evening, embark on a Gondola Serenade.

• Enjoy a wine-happy evening, revelling with musicians who perform all those Italian songs and light operatic favourites which great-grandma knew and loved.

3.2 Beyond the historic centre

What next, after you've seen the great highlights around St Mark's Square? There are dozens of museums and galleries to explore, an incredible 900 palaces to admire, and magnificent churches around every corner.

All that, amid a visual feast which supported whole generations of artists, who busily painted the Venetian panorama for centuries... With camera along the Grand Canal, you can repeat this scenic dream-world, quite unchanged from the early 18th-century paintings of Canaletto.

To top up your sightseeing, browse through the later chapters in this book. Local travel agencies link some of the suggestions into a supplementary guided tour by foot and gondola. Otherwise you can compile your own package, using the water bus services.

Plentiful choice will still remain, to fill your next-time visit.

There's also great delight in making your own discoveries, getting lost amid the maze of narrow canals, and exploring mysterious alleys that lead into peaceful little squares.

At every unexpected turning there's another sleepy picture of a Venice which is little changed from the days of the great painters.

3.3 Sunday in Venice

Venice becomes very busy on a Sunday, as all the mainlanders come over to Venice in their Sunday best for the 'Passeggiata'. There are often special events on a Sunday. Check in Venice for the details.

Shops & Markets
Most clothes shops are closed on a Sunday, but many gift stores are open, selling Venetian glass or Burano lace. These shops are mostly grouped in the St Mark's Square area, around the Rialto Bridge and near the Lista di Spagna that leads from the Railway Station – one of the more economical shopping districts.

Museums & Galleries
Most of the museums and galleries are open on Sundays – at least until lunchtime. See 'Museums & Galleries' section for further details.

Church Services
Services are usually held in Italian, but occasionally the Church of St Moise behind St Mark's Square has a service in English.

The Basilica of St Mark's has a sung mass at 10.00 hrs.

The Anglican Church is located near the Accademia, at Campo San Vio 870. Services are held at 8.30 hrs and 11.00 hrs; Matins 10.30 hrs.

Your representative can provide you with full details of other services in English.

Chapter Four
The great highlights

4.1 Around St Mark's Square

All Venetian sightseeing starts at St Mark's Square, on foot. The essentials can be covered by the go-it-alone traveller with a guide-book. But you'd probably miss many of the details. It's worth taking a preliminary tour with a guide who has probably been doing the circuit for years, bringing the highlights to life. Just a reminder: modest dress is required for entry to the Cathedral – and, indeed, to other churches in Venice.

Here is Basic Venice in one easy walk.

Piazza San Marco

Napoleon called St Mark's Square "the most splendid drawing-room in Europe." The Piazza could easily win the popular vote for the world's most beautiful square. Paved with marble, this focal-point of Venice is about 190 yards long by 90 yards wide, with colonnades each side and enclosed at the end by the gorgeous facade of St Mark's.

Thousands of pigeons have traditional squatting-rights, and are fed at public expense. Peddlers sell bird-seed, and the pigeons earn their extra rations by perching on your shoulder or in your hair for that essential photograph with St Mark's in the background.

Expensive cafés with music enable you to enjoy the whole fabulous scene: flower sellers, instant-portrait artists, crocodiles of tourists, all in this wonderful setting of breath-taking architecture. In the arcades are shops to make you drool.

The Bell Tower (Campanile)

325 feet high, the Campanile dominates Piazza San Marco. It was completely rebuilt in 1912 after the original 1100-year-old building collapsed in 1802. There's a lift, entrance fee 5,000 lire. Open: Daily – Summer 9.30-19.30 hrs; Winter 10-16 hrs.

The Piazzetta

This smaller square opens out from Piazza S. Marco onto the quayside which looks across to the island of S. Giorgio Maggiore. The Piazzetta has the Doge's Palace to one side, faced by the Libreria Vecchia on the other.

The Old Library was rated by Palladio as the most beautiful building since antiquity. It houses the 'Library of St Mark', though the 700,000 volumes have overflowed into the adjoining Mint (Zecca).

The twin columns of St Theodore and St Mark were removed from Lebanon in 1125. The winged Lion of St Mark – universal symbol of Venetian power – probably came originally from Persia.

According to Venetian superstition it's bad luck to walk between the two columns, where public executions formerly took place. But most visitors are blissfully unaware.

Here is a popular departure point for boat tours, and gondoliers are always alert for romantic-looking couples who could be persuaded into a 50-minute cruise without checking the price first.

The Clock Tower (Torre dell'Orologio)

This 15th-century tower stands on St Mark's Square to the left of the Cathedral. Besides telling the time, the complicated clock face also shows phases of the moon and signs of the zodiac. Two bronze Moors deafen everyone assembled in the square by hammering on the bell every hour. They have hammered out the time since 1497. Access to the Tower is closed for restoration. Check whether entry is yet possible.

The archway beneath is entrance to the main shopping street called Merceria, which zig-zags through to Rialto Bridge – well signposted en route.

4.2 Saint Mark's Cathedral

The Basilica di San Marco is 'the' great place to see in Venice – the Basilica built to enshrine the body of St Mark, stolen in 9th century from his tomb in Alexandria. It was a shrewd robbery, giving Venice great prestige, second only to Rome, and basis of a lucrative pilgrim trade. The present Greek-cross ground-plan with five domes was built in 11th century. The golden mosaics were added in 12th and 13th centuries, with dazzling upgrades by Renaissance artists such as Titian and Tintoretto. Visit the Galleria above, for a closer view.

The interior is a treasure house, thanks partly to an edict dated 1075 that all Venetian trading vessels should bring back from their voyage something of value to enrich the Basilica. Hence the hundreds of rare marble columns, and items of alabaster and jasper. The Treasury is crammed with 4th-Crusade booty from Constantinople. Greek, Byzantine, medieval, Tuscan, Lombard and Venetian art have all left their mark, to make the Cathedral a sumptuous museum.

The golden altar-piece called the Pala d'Oro, encrusted with jewels and depicting scenes from St Mark's life, is the product of 500 years' of local craftsmanship. The famous four Bronze Horses on the terrace above the main door are copies. The originals – more loot from Constantinople – are inside the Cathedral, to protect them from 20th-century pollution.
Masses: Sunday at 7.00, 7.45, 8.30, 9.15, 10.00 & 18.45 hrs. Sung Mass: 10.00 hrs.

4.3 Doge's Palace

The Palazzo Ducale adjoining St Mark's Basilica is the former residence of the Doges, and seat of Government during the Venetian Republic. This is the most fantastic public residence of all time – a treasure house of Venetian painting, with every great Renaissance artist represented.

The Giants' Staircase is named after Sansovino's huge statues of Neptune and Mars, symbols of Venetian power on sea and land.

Council chamber

Specially interesting are the private apartments of the Doges, and the massive 14th-century Hall of the Great Council, which could accommodate up to 1800 registered voters who could attend the Council sessions. Here's where all the big decisions were made.

Italy's finest artists all had a share in painting the Hall, though many originals were destroyed by fire in 1577. Tintoretto, Veronese, Bassano and Palma the Younger decorated the reconstructed building. Tintoretto's main contribution was *Paradise*, claimed as the world's largest oil painting, measuring 72 feet by 22.

In contrast to all this opulence, you can visit the dungeons and torture chambers which backed up the administration of justice.

Bridge of Sighs (Il Ponte dei Sospiri)

Walk along the side of the Doge's Palace, facing out to the Lagoon. Look down the first side-canal – Rio del Pallazo – and there's the famous Bridge of Sighs which connects the Doge's Palace with the prison across the canal. Among the most famous inmates was Casanova, who managed to escape.

Chapter Five

Beyond the centre

5.1 Sightseeing by Vaporetti

Out of the 118 Venetian islands, most have a parish church or two and a civic square to make a focal point for each community.

But for purposes of administration the city splits into six districts called *sestieri* – San Marco, Castello and Cannaregio on one side of the Grand Canal; Santa Croce, San Polo and Dorsoduro (which takes in Giudecca and San Giorgio) on the western side.

The great highlights are concentrated in the historic centre of San Marco, and all along the Grand Canal itself. Most short-time visitors concentrate on those two areas. However, there is rewarding sightseeing in the off-trail sectors of the city, where time-consuming navigation may be needed to locate specific targets.

Much of the supplementary sightseeing can be done with help of the Vaporetti services, which place you within easy walking distance of the numbered bus-stop.

Every journey itself is a major sightseeing bonus, giving you photo subjects all the way. It's worth packing a long-focus lens to capture some of the fascinating details of buildings and traffic along the canals.

Many of the great palaces along the Grand Canal have been converted into museums – see Chapter Seven for details, and for access by water-bus. But also a number of churches are worth visiting, either for their history and architecture or for works of art by great painters of the Venetian school.

5.2 A selection of churches

Santa Maria della Salute

Built in thanksgiving for the ending of a plague in 1631, when 40,000 died in Venice alone. November 21 is still kept as a public holiday, to commemorate deliverance from the plague. The architectural plan is octagonal, and there are two huge domes. The sacristy contains twelve paintings by Titian, and the *Marriage at Cana* by Tintoretto.

Water Bus: 1. Stop: no. 14 – Salute.

Santa Maria Gloriosa dei Frari

Campo San Rocco

A Franciscan Gothic-style church, built in 14th century. The campanile is the second highest in Venice.

Many famous Venetians are buried here, including Titian. Over the High Altar is one of Titian's greatest religious paintings – the *Assumption*.

Water bus 1. Stop: no. 10 – San Tomà.

San Polo (San Paolo)

Campo di San Polo

One of the city's oldest churches. Contains several important works by famous Venetian artists, including Tintoretto and Tiepolo.

Water Bus: 1. Stop: no. 8 – San Silvestro.

San Giorgio Maggiore

Basilica on the island of San Giorgio Maggiore, built 1791 by Palladio. From the bell tower – lift available – there's a splendid view across to St. Mark's Square.

The church contains two Tintorettos.

Water Bus: 52 from Zaccaria – one stop to S. Giorgio.

Santa Maria Formosa

Located north of St. Mark's, and due east of Rialto Bridge, on a lively square called Campo Santa Maria Formosa, with a regular morning fruit market. The church dates from the 7th century when the Virgin Mary is reputed to have appeared to the Venetians as a fully-formed lady (Formosa). The present church was rebuilt in 1492.

San Zanipolo (Santi Giovanni e Paolo)

Located a few blocks north again of Santa Maria Formosa (see above)
One of the finest Gothic churches in Venice. Contains a beautiful altarpiece by Giovanni Bellini, and four ceiling paintings by Veronese.

5.3 Jewish Museum

Campo del Ghetto Nuova, Cannaregio Tel: 715012
Notice that word 'ghetto'? It's the original Venetian word, used in its modern sense since 1555, when a Papal decree enforced the medieval principle of segregation into a defined city area. Napoleon lifted the restriction when he defeated the Venetian Republic in 1797. In this ancient centre – near the present-day railway station – were five synagogues, mostly Ashkenazi.

The museum documents Jewish history in Venice since the original 11th-century settlement on the island of Giudecca. It also includes a wide variety of traditional Jewish art during the 17th to 19th centuries.
Open: 10.00-16.30 hrs. Closed: Sat and Jewish holidays. Entry: 4,000 lire, or guided visit 10,000 lire. Water Bus: 52. Stop: Ponte delle Guglie.

5.4 Parks and gardens

Giardinetti
Molo, Quay San Marco
This small park adds a touch of green, which is otherwise lacking in the city.

Giardini Pubblici (Public Gardens)
Riva dei sette Martiri
The gardens were laid out on the instructions of Napoleon 1, at the South East of the main island.

The towering Campanile in Piazza San Marco.

Piazza San Marco provides a magnificent meeting place for both tourists and locals.

The Grand Canal at sunset.

The Rialto Bridge, the geographical centre of the city, has been a focal point of Venetian commerce for centuries.

Dining at a waterside restaurant - a typically romantic Venetian experience.

Gondoliers in traditional dress.

Unmistakably Venice.

Chapter Six

Around the Lagoon

6.1 The Lido

When you want a break from dedicated sightseeing, it's worth taking a breezy boat-ride to the Lido or some of the other islands of the Venetian Lagoon.

The Lido is a narrow strip of land which acts as a natural dyke, protecting the Lagoon from the winter storms and high tides of the Adriatic. As a helping hand to Nature, a massive sea wall was built in the second half of the 18th century.

From the arrival landing-stage, a short walk along a boulevard lined with trees, cafés and souvenir vendors brings you to the Adriatic beach.

The Lido has had its share of world history. In 1202, thirty thousand knights from all over Europe assembled here before launching themselves into the Fourth Crusade. They waited while their leaders and the Venetians haggled over the transport cost.

Nineteenth-century poets put the Lido on the map for romantic escapists. Shelley, Byron and Goethe were among those who recognised the Lido's attractions. Byron converted a derelict fort into stables, and took regular gallops along the sands.

During the past hundred years, the Lido has flourished as a resort in its own right, with luxury hotels, and top-grade summer-season entertainment in the Casino.

The adjacent Palazzo del Cinema hosts the famous Film Festival in late August and early September: a great time for star-gazing.

Access to the beach is high-cost in the prime areas, but free each end of the island.

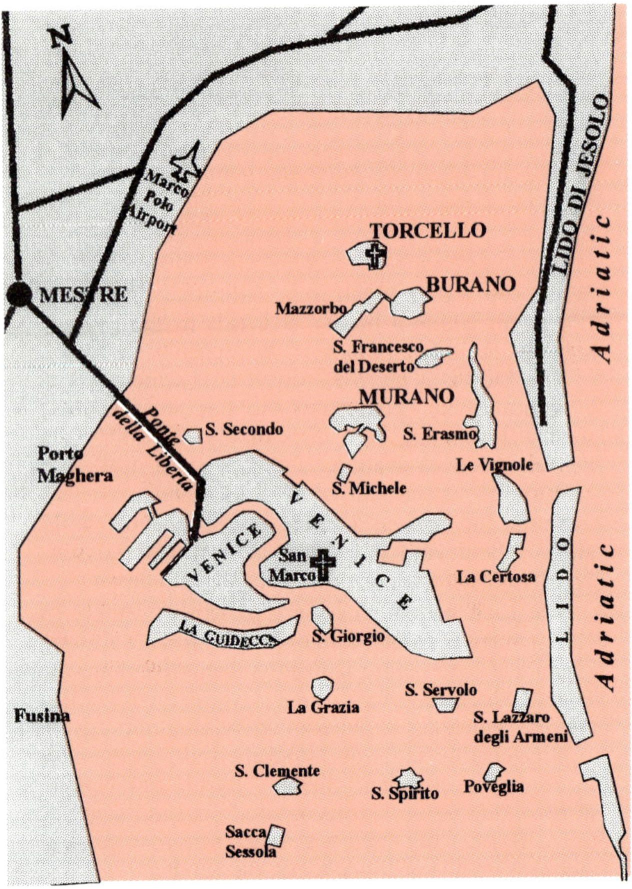

N

MESTRE

Marco Polo Airport

TORCELLO

BURANO

Mazzorbo

S. Francesco del Deserto

MURANO

S. Secondo

S. Erasmo

Porto Maghera

Ponte della Libertà

Le Vignole

S. Michele

V E N I C E

V E N I C E

San Marco

La Certosa

VENICE

LA GIUDECCA

S. Giorgio

Fusina

S. Servolo

La Grazia

S. Lazzaro degli Armeni

S. Clemente

S. Spirito

Poveglia

Sacca Sessola

LIDO DI JESOLO

Adriatic

LIDO

Adriatic

THE VENETIAN LAGOON

0   km   2

6.2 Murano and San Michele

Some glass stores near St Mark's Square set aside a small workshop where craftsmen display their traditional skills. To visit an authentic glassworks, take a boat to the island of Murano, where furnaces have been in full blast since 1291. The industry was moved there, to avoid the fire risk to Venice itself.

On arrival at the Murano jetty, visitors are escorted by guides to watch glass-blowing in one of the numerous establishments. Needless to say, there is ample opportunity to buy products that range from kitsch to high quality.

But there's no hard sell, as enough visitors buy to make the hospitality worth while. It's hard to compare like with like, but prices are little different from the shops of central Venice.

Murano's long history as a highly skilled centre for production of spectacles, mirrors and coloured crystal is displayed in the Glass Museum – Museo Vetrario. (Open daily except Wed, 10-17 hrs; entrance 8,000 lire.) The same ticket also is valid for the Modern and Contemporary Glass Museum, filled with highly imaginative international work.

Some water buses stop at the cemetery island of San Michele, which has its fascination for those who like to see the graves of notabilities such as Stravinsky, Diaghilev and Ezra Pound.

6.3 Torcello and Burano

For an excursion requiring much more time, the colourful island of Burano is a fishing community with the menfolk catching clams – *vongole* – while the women make exquisite lace. A Lace Museum records the history of Burano lace-making.

Neighbouring Torcello is now virtually depopulated. But two fine churches – a cathedral dating from 1008 but founded in 639, and the 11th-century Santa Fosca – are a reminder that Torcello was the first island in the Lagoon to be settled by 5th-century refugees from the mainland.

Chapter Seven

Museums and Galleries

7.1 Opening times

Note: Opening times and closing days of Museums and Galleries in Venice are a law unto themselves. Before planning a visit, please check locally for the latest information and entrance fees. Opening times can vary greatly during winter months.

Staff problems or renovations can disrupt opening times, or close off entire sections of great museums, sometimes for years on end. Most museums close one day a week, usually either on Monday or Tuesday. Before making a special journey across Venice, check the current opening hours.

Caution: on the principal public holidays, virtually all shops, museums and galleries are closed.

Entrance fees range from about 3,000 to 12,000 lire. These are also liable to change, though not dramatically. Quoted fees can serve as a guideline. Some age-related discounts may be available.

Academy, Ponte dell'Accademia   Tel: 5222247

This museum ranks as the world's finest collection of 14th to 18th century Venetian painting. Make this gallery your top choice, if you cannot work round all the others.

Converted from three religious buildings, the Academy Gallery centres around Tintoretto, Giorgioni, the Bellini family, Veronese, Titian, Guardi, Canaletto and Tiepolo. It's a rich feast, giving you a total survey of the greatest Venetian painters.

Open: 9-19 hrs. Entrance 12,000 lire.

Water Bus: 1. Stop: no. 12 – Accademia.

The Peggy Guggenheim Collection

Dorsoduro 701   Tel: 5206288
Palazzo Venier dei Leoni, on Grand Canal halfway
between Santa Maria della Salute and the Accademia.

Houses a magnificent private collection of 20th
century art, featuring Cubist, Abstract and Surrealist sculptures and paintings assembled by the American heiress.

Most of the big 20th-century names are represented, from Picasso, Braque and Chagall to postwar artists such as Francis Bacon, Pollock and
Sutherland.

The collection is maybe not of the same incomparable quality of the Guggenheim in New York
City. But it's still worth the boat-ride.

Open: Daily except Tuesday, 11-18 hrs.
Water Bus: 1. Stop: no. 12 – Accademia.
Entrance: 10,000 lire.

Ca' d'Oro and the Franchetti Gallery

Ca' d'Oro   Tel: 5238790
A miracle of 15th-century Venetian Gothic – a patrician dwelling, beautifully restored after flood
damage. From the first floor loggia, enjoy beautiful
views of the Grand Canal.

The palace houses the Galleria Franchetti collection of tapestries, sculptures and paintings, including works by Carpaccio, Titian and Van Dyck.

Open: 9-14 hrs. Entrance: 4,000 lire.
Water Bus: 1. Stop: no. 6 – Ca' d'Oro.

Scuola Grande di San Rocco

Campo San Rocco, next to the Frari Tel: 5234864
A 16th-century white marble building with its upper
hall decorated by a magnificent cycle of paintings
of Old and New Testament scenes by Tintoretto.
Among other Tintorettos in the collection is his
great masterpiece, the *Crucifixion*. Evening concerts
are often held in the main hall. During the interval,
the audience may visit other halls in the school.

Open: 9-17.30 hrs; Closed Mon. Entrance: 8,000
lire. Water Bus: 1. Stop: no. 10 – San Tomà.

Modern Art Museum Ca'Pesaro

Palazzo Pesaro, Santa Croce   Tel: 721127
This gallery, housed in a 17th-century Venetian Baroque palace, features 19th and 20th century paintings by both Italian and foreign artists.
Open: 10-16 hrs except Mon. Entrance 5,000 lire. Check first whether still closed for restoration.
Water Bus: 1. Stop: no. 5 – S. Staè.

Museum of Oriental Art

Santa Croce Ca' Pesaro   Tel: 5241173
On the third floor of the Palazzo Pesaro (see previous entry)
An excellent collection of oriental vases, furnishings, paintings, sculpture and weapons – mainly from China, Japan and India.
Open: Tue-Sun 9-14 hrs.
Water Bus: 1. Stop: no. 5 – S. Staè. Entrance: 4,000 lire.

Correr Museum

Piazza di San Marco   Tel: 5225625
Located at the opposite end of the Piazza from St Mark's Cathedral.
    Contains documents, records and antique relics of the life of Venice from the 14th to the 18th centuries; and also a rich collection of paintings from 14th to 16th century.
    The museum's most famous work is *Christ giving the keys to St Peter* by Lorenzo Veneziano. Here also is Carpaccio's *Two Venetian Ladies*, otherwise known as *The Courtesans*.
Open: Summer 9-19 hrs.
Entrance: 8,000 lire, or 14,000 lire as a combined ticket with Doge's Palace.

Museo del Risorgimento, 800 Veneziano

Located on the second floor of Correr Museum (see previous entry)
    Covers the history of Venice from 700 AD to 1866 (the fall of the Republic).
Open: Mon-Sat 10-16 hrs. Closed Tuesday. Sun 9-12.30 hrs.

Scuola di San Giorgio degli Schiavoni

Castello 3259; on Calle dei Furlani – from Riva degli Schiavoni, at the fourth bridge up Rio della Pietà.   Tel: 5228828

This museum is well worth the effort of finding what was the former headquarters of Dalmatian traders. The ground floor exhibition displays a series of early 16th-century paintings by Carpaccio, illustrating lives of three patron Saints of Dalmatia – George, Trifone and Jerome.

The scenes vividly depict 16th-century life in the Venice region.

Open: Tue-Sat 10-12.30 & 15-18 hrs. Sun 10-12.30 hrs. Entrance: 5,000 lire. Water Bus: 1, 82 or 52. Stop: no. 16 – San Zaccaria.

Museum of the Settecento (Palazzo Rezzonico)

Ca'Rezzonico (S. Barnaba)   Tel: 2418506
One of the most splendid examples of 18th-century Venetian Rococo style – a palace built by wealthy Genoese bankers called Rezzonico. The finest artists were commissioned for the decorations.

Robert Browning died here in 1889, during a visit to his son who had earlier bought the Palace (after marrying an American heiress).

The elaborate furnishings, tapestries, decorations and paintings are all 18th century.

Open: Sun-Thu 10-19 hrs; Fri-Sat 10-22 hrs. Entrance: 12,000 lire.
Water Bus: 1. Stop: no. 11 – Ca'Rezzonico.

Museum of St Mark's Basilica   Tel: 5225205

Piazza San Marco
The Marciano Museum is located on the upper floors of St Mark's Basilica.

On display are carpets and tapestries, religious ornaments and precious items which belong to the Basilica.

The principal reason for climbing up the steep staircase is to get a close-up view of the original four horses and chariot which were removed from the Basilica terrace because of the pollution risk.

Open: 9.30-17.30 hrs. Entrance: 3,000 lire.

MUSEUMS

Museum Fortuny

S Beneto 3780   Tel: 5200995

Set in the Gothic palace which belonged to the Pesaro family, the museum contains works by Mariano Fortuny, famed for Fortuny silks. The collection includes paintings, fabrics, furniture and photographs.
Open: Tue-Sun 8.30-13.30 hrs. Entrance: 4,000 lire. Check first whether still closed for restoration.
Water Bus: 1. Stop: no. 9 – San Angelo.

Museum of Icons and Hellenic Study

Castello 3412   Tel: 5226581

Housed in the Scuola di San Niccolò dei Greci, this museum contains the famous Greek codices which include three Byzantine gospels of the 13th and 14th century, eighty icons from the Byzantine period, and works of Cretan and Greek artists who settled in Venice.
Open: Mon-Sat 9-13 & 14-17 hrs; Sun 9-12.30 hrs. Closed Tuesday.
Water Bus: 1. Stop: no. 16 – San Zaccaria. Entrance: 3,000 lire.

Museum of Natural History,   Tel: 5240885

Fondaco dei Turchi, Santa Croce 1730

A Grand Canal palace founded early 13th century. It later functioned as a tobacco warehouse and residence for Turkish traders, and was converted to a museum in 1880. Main attraction is the science room with two Basilisks (mythological animals made up of the parts of other animals). The Dinosaur room is a must.
Open: Tue-Sun 9-13 hrs. Check first whether still closed for restoration. Entrance: 5,000 lire.
Water Bus: 1. Stop: no. 3 – Riva di Biagio.

Chapter Eight

Go shopping

8.1 Glass galore

Shopping for the standard tourist purchases is far easier in Venice than in other major cities.

Florence is best for leather; Milan for silk; and Rome or Naples for gloves. But all those specialities and other craft products like cameos or lace are available, in infinite variety, in the hundreds of stores that line the narrow streets of Venice.

Comparison shopping is easy, with a dozen similar window-displays within a hundred yards. Haggling can bring price reductions, especially in late season when shopkeepers want to clear their shelves for the winter recess.

Venetian glass comes in wonderful, glittering array, with highest prices in the arcades of St Mark's Square itself. Best bargains are in small glassware shops away from the centre. It's fascinating to take a boat excursion to see glass-blowers at work on the island of Murano, but prices in the factory showrooms are not necessarily any cheaper.

From street stalls you can often buy very low-cost figurines which are slightly sub-standard, with flaws that only an expert would detect.

Other interesting buys:

Leather – fabulous choice! Jackets, trousers, skirts, shoes, gloves.

Silks – a great selection of ties, scarves and shirts. The patterns and colours are full of sunny Italy.

Lace – is mostly handmade in Burano, or specially imported from Korea or Taiwan. Try and tell the difference, apart from the price!

SHOPPING

Masks – are a revival from the age of masked balls, a key part of Venetian culture. Banned for many years, masks are again hand-made specially for Carnival celebrations in February. In olden times, Venetian brides wore masks on their wedding day.

8.2 Shopping districts

Opening hours are generally 9.00-12.30 and 15.00-19.30 hrs. Closed Sunday, and Monday morning.

San Marco area – The luxury end of Venetian trade is around the arcades of Piazza San Marco, and along the streets just west of the Piazza. Just look at the fabulous window displays, but don't dare ask the prices if you cannot stand shocks.

The Merceria – One of Europe's most famous shopping streets, following a narrow and zigzag route between St Mark's Square (starting from the archway below the Clock Tower) to the Rialto Bridge.

Shops are full of designer clothes, including leather goods created by famous names such as Fendi, Armani, Gucci, Al Duca d'Aosto, Gianni Versace, Bussola...

The Rialto Bridge – The bridge itself, and the area just north, is crowded with tiny shops that sell jewellery, lace, handbags, gloves and many knickknacks.

Allow plenty of time for strolling, but **remember that this is ideal pickpocket territory**.

Markets

Venetian markets are open generally from very early morning until about 14.00 hrs. Closed Sundays.

Fabbriche Nuove, on Grand Canal, just north-west of Rialto

This fishmarket is famous for its variety of Adriatic seafood such as eels, crabs, scampi, octopus, mussels and sea bass. The area is also well supplied with excellent cheese kiosks. The views across the Grand Canal are superb.

Rio Terra San Leonardo, over Ponte delle Guglie
A very colourful fruit and veg market, open daily.

Street stalls are everywhere. The fruit and vegetable vendors sell melons, peaches, artichokes, grapes, mushrooms, oranges, and it's even possible to buy a five-kilo drum of Parmesan cheese.

In the main sightseeing areas, souvenir vendors are numerous and persistent. Low-cost souvenirs are often claimed as genuine hand-crafted Italian, but could be mass-produced. Cheap cameos offered by street dealers are likely to be plastic.

8.3 Clothing Sizes

There is no exact science about conversions between British, American and Italian clothing sizes. The following figures offer some guidance as a prelude to trying on garments before purchase.

Women's dresses and suits

British	32	34	36	38	40	42
or British	6	8	10	12	14	16
USA	4	6	8	10	12	14
Italian	38	40	42	44	46	48

Men's suits and coats

UK & USA	36	38	40	42	44	46
Italian	46	48	50	52	54	56

Men's Shirts

UK & USA	14½	15	15½	16	16½	17
Italian	37	38	39	40	42	43

Women's Shoes

UK	2	3	4	5	6	7	8
USA	3	4	5	6	7	8	9
Italian	34	36	37	38	39	40	41

Men's Shoes

UK	5	6	7	8	9	10	11
USA	6	7	8	9	10	11	12
Italian	38	39	41	42	43	44	46

Chapter Nine

Nightlife in Venice

9.1 The romance industry

It's Romance that balances the Venetian budget: the Romance of a medieval past, and of moonlight on the Lagoon. After dark, gondoliers light their coloured lanterns in readiness for the loving-couple trade. An hour of Venice by Night – along mysterious, dimly-lit canals, and preferably with music – is essential to any well-organised honeymoon.

If you want music with your gondola, you hire a singer and instrumentalist for the appropriate extra fee. On a personalised basis, that will cost a fortune. However, the cost can be kept within decent limits by taking an organised Gondola Serenade. Six persons to a gondola, a flotilla sets off, keeping close to another boat with the quota of musicians.

Certainly, after a full day of museums and churches, it's time to relax. In general, Venetian nightlife consists of dining in leisurely style, and then sitting at an outdoor café, watching the world go by. For more action, certain restaurants offer entertainment; there's a handful of discos; and the Casino. Depending on the season, the theatre may offer an alternative. Watch posters for what's on.

9.2 Restaurants with entertainment

Prices are usually quite high. Check them out before dining. Or ask your rep about a 'Venetian Experience' that includes a typical Venetian meal with sparkling wine and 1½ hours of song. **Ai Musicanti** is housed in a 17th-century palace.

Antico Pignolo, Calle Specchieri 451

L'Arlecchino, Hotel Bauer Grünwald, San Moise 1440

Les Deux Lions, Riva degli Schiavoni

Tel: 5200533

Night Club Antico Martini, San Marco, Campo San Fantin 1980

Parco delle Rose, Lido

9.3 Theatres

La Fenice, one of Italy's great 19th-century opera houses where premieres by Rossini, Verdi, Bellini and Benjamin Britten were performed, was demolished by fire in January 1996. It is currently being rebuilt. Meanwhile performances are staged on the Island of Tronchetto, the car park island.

Chamber and orchestral concerts are given in a variety of churches and other venues.

Del Ridotto, Calle Ca'Vallaresso, San Marco

Tel: 22939

Malibran, Cannaregio 5870

Goldoni, Calle Goldoni   Tel: 705838

9.4 Venice Casino

From mid-September to mid-June, the Palazzo Vendramin houses the Venice Casino. It's here that Richard Wagner lived when he composed *Tristan and Isolde*. Water bus 1, stop 4 (San Marcuolo).

In the peak summer months the casino operation moves to the Lido. In both locations there are floorshows, restaurants and dancing. You can play roulette, chemin de fer, baccarat, blackjack and slot machines. Jacket and tie are required for gentlemen. Remember to take your passport to gain admittance to the gambling rooms.

Open from 4 p.m. until 3 a.m. Entrance fee: 15,000 lire Lido; 25,000 lire Venice.

Chapter Ten
Learn Italian

Don't worry if you cannot speak Italian. In the main hotels, restaurants, bars and shops, service staff have at least a smattering of most West European languages. If not, there's always someone handy who can translate.

However, there's pleasure in being able to use and recognise even just a few words. It's even easier if you have some basic French or Spanish. Pronunciation is reasonably phonetic.

The following letters are pronounced as in English: *b, d, f, l, m, n, t, v.*

For the vowels, pronounce:

a as in English p*a*st;

e has two sounds – as in p*e*st or p*a*ste;

i as in pr*i*est;

o has two sounds – as in p*o*st or p*o*t;

u as in b*oo*st.

The tricky consonants are:

c as in *ch*ase or *ch*eese before *e* and *i*;

  as in *c*ast, *c*ost or *c*oot before *a, o* or *u*.

g as in *g*ender or *g*enes before *e* and *i*;

  as in *g*arnish, *g*olf or *g*oose before *a, o* or *u*.

z has two sounds – as in mai*ds* or as in ba*ts*.

Some consonants are twinned for special effects:

ch before *e* or *i* becomes hard like a *k*.

gh before *e* or *i* becomes hard as in *gh*etto.

gl before *i* becomes liquid as in bi*lli*ards.

gn before all vowels is pronounced as in o*ni*on.

qu as in *qu*ality.

The Italian language does not use *k, w, x* or *y.*

For the beginner in Italian, we give a starter kit of a few words to show you're trying.

Greetings

Good morning	Buon giorno
Good afternoon	Buon pomeriggio
Good evening	Buona sera
How are you?	Come sta?
Very well, thank you	Benissimo, grazie
Goodbye	Arrivederci!
Good night	Buona notte

The essentials

Yes	Sì
No	No
Please	Per favore
Thank you	Grazie
Don't mention it	Prego
Excuse me! (on bus, etc)	Permesso!
Do you speak English?	Parla inglese?
I don't understand	Non capisco
At what time?	A che ora?

Money

Where is the bank?	Dov'è la banca?
Currency exchange	Cambio
I want to change $50.	Desidero cambiare cinquanta dollari.
How much is this?	Quanto costa questo?
Something cheaper	Qualcosa più a buon mercato
Too expensive!	Troppo caro!

Shopping

Chemist	la farmacia
Doctor	il medico; dottore
Hairdresser	parrucchiere
Post office	ufficio postale
Supermarket	supermercato
Tobacconist	la tabaccheria
I want to buy…	Voglio comprare…
a city map	una cartina della città
some cigarettes	delle sigarette
some stamps	dei francobolli
postcards	cartoline postali
English newspapers	giornali inglesi

LEARN ITALIAN

Sightseeing

Where is the ...?	Dov'è ... ?
bridge	il ponte
church	la chiesa
museum	il museo
palace	il palazzo
square	la piazza
station	la stazione
Turn left, right	volti a sinistra, destra
Go straight ahead	vada diritto
Is it open on Sundays?	È aperto la domenica?
When was it built?	Quando fu costuito?

Days of the week

Monday to Sunday – Lunedì, martedì, mercoledì, gioverdì, venerdì, sabato, domenica.

Today	oggi
Tomorrow	domani
Yesterday	ieri

Months

January to December – gennaio, febbraio, marzo, aprile, maggio, giugno, luglio, agosto, settembre, ottobre, novembre, dicembre.

Numbers

0	zero		
1-10	uno, due, tre, quattro, cinque, sei, sette, otto,nove, dieci		
11-19	undici, dodici, tredici, quattordici, quindici, sedici, diciasette, diciotto, diciannove		
20-29	venti, ventuno, ventidue, ventitre etc.		
30-39	trenta, trentuno, trentadue etc.		
40-90	quaranta, cinquanta, sessanta, settanta, ottanta, novanta		
100	cento	101	centouno
143	centoquarantatre	200	duecento
1000	mille	2000	duemila
1,000,000	un milione		
First, second, third		primo, secondo, terzo	

The menu: Please see the next chapter for a food and drink vocabulary.

Chapter Eleven

Eating and drinking

11.1 Dining out in Venice

Venetians are great food-lovers, and certainly like to take their time. Lunch or dinner can last at least two hours over three or more courses.

For much of the year you can dine outdoors, enjoying both the food and what's happening around you. Excellent seafood is available everywhere, but is not necessarily cheap.

Although prices for à la carte meals can be rather high, most establishments also feature set fixed-price menus with good choice at each course. Besides the pricier restaurants, there are many more modest places which offer tasty meals at reasonable cost. Try them for a simple lunch.

Venice can be enjoyed sitting down, in hundreds of locations – not just in St Mark's Square. The Venetians spend much of their ample off-season leisure at canalside cafés, gossiping and watching the world float by. Favourite drinks are tiny, extra-strong cups of Espresso coffee, or apéritifs like Campari soda.

Just like everywhere else in Italy, Venice has colourful restaurants by the hundred. It's worth devoting a good part of your City Break funds to the enjoyment of good food in surroundings that are loaded with atmosphere.

If you go overboard for Italian cuisine with Italian wine, you can have glorious eating at almost any side-canal establishment. It's much more fun than eating standard 'international' hotel menus. Don't worry if you cannot speak Italian - just wave and point. But most waiters have basic English.

DINING OUT

Restaurant choice

Italy features three main kinds of restaurant – *osteria*, *trattoria* and *ristorante*, in ascending order of quality and price, though nowadays the distinction is blurring.

If you cannot manage a full meal at lunch-time, there are plenty of chances for snacks. Many bars have a selection of sandwiches called *tramezzini* which have very appetising fillings.

There's another type of restaurant/café called *tavola calda*, where you can get simple hot dishes at reasonable price. They are many of them in Venice. Customers eat standing up – dishes of spaghetti, ravioli or whatever the dish of the day happens to be. It's very handy for a quick lunch, if you don't want a full sit-down meal spread over a couple of hours.

At a pizzeria, you can fill up with a bowl of thick minestrone and a huge pizza that overlaps a dinner plate.

For picnic eating, there is good, cheap fruit - oranges, cherries, melons, peaches, apricots, grapes, fresh figs, according to season. Excellent cheeses, cooked meats and salads help keep outgoings low.

Learn the Italian word *etto*, which means hectogramme or 100 grammes. For quick guidance, reckon it's a quarter-pound or four ounces. Fish or steak dishes are frequently priced per *etto*, not per portion. Know the system, and save yourself a nasty shock when the bill comes.

Quick snacks

There is something very typically Italian about the snack bars dominated by a massive Espresso machine, gleaming and polished and steaming. On the shelves behind are bottles of every conceivable spirit and liqueur known to European man. These establishments are also useful as a stopping-point for a quick sandwich.

In the mornings from 7 to 11 a.m. you'll find Italians having their breakfasts of cappuccinos and cornettos (croissants). However, if you feel in need of a brandy, you will not be on your own!

Bar codes

If you take a drink at the bar, you must normally pay first at the cash desk (cassa). Take the receipt to the bar, and tell the barman what you want. A small tip can ensure rapid service. Standing at the bar is always much cheaper than having drinks and sandwiches served to a table. You're not supposed to buck the system by ordering at the bar, and then sitting down.

In restaurants, a standard 'menu turistico' comprises a flat-rate 3-course menu, usually with a drink such as beer or quarter-litre of wine, service and tax. The price may be reasonable enough, but don't expect any gastronomic highlights.

Most restaurants charge 'coperto', which is a cover charge of about 3,000 lire per person. Then there is service which can add 10-20% on the total bill. Tipping is not necessary on top, unless for exceptional service. VAT is added. Keep the bill, as tax inspectors are making valiant attempts to keep tabs on the catering trade. Within 200 metres of a restaurant, inspectors can ask you to produce your receipt: otherwise, a hefty fine. However, for the foreign tourist, it's all rather theoretical.

11.2 Plenty of Pasta

In Italy you can eat pasta twice a day during a one-week City Break, and come nowhere near repeating yourself. The variations on the pasta theme are enormous. It comes mainly in two colours: the usual cream colour; and green, made by working spinach into the paste. It's also made in a huge variety of shapes. Lifetime students of pasta break down mamma's favourite food into five groups:

- Rope or string, e.g. Spaghetti
- Ribbon, e.g. Tagliatelle
- Tubes, e.g. Penne
- Envelopes, e.g. Ravioli
- Fancy shapes like shells or wheels, such as Conchiglie, Tortellini.

Pasta short-list

Agnolotti/ Anolini	Small stuffed envelopes, like ravioli
Cannelloni	Large tubes, stuffed with various meat or vegetables, and baked in cheese and tomato sauce
Cappelletti	Twists of pasta, usually stuffed and served in a light sauce. Another version of tortellini.
Conchiglie	Shell-shaped pasta
Farfalloni	Pasta in the shape of a butterfly
Fettuccine	Thin ribbon pasta made with egg. The Roman name for tagliatelle.
Fusilli	Skeins of ribbon pasta
Lasagne	Ribbon pasta, usually baked after boiling
Lasagne verdi	Green lasagne
Penne	Small tubes
Pastina	Small, fine pasta in a variety of shapes for soup
Ravioli	Small envelopes, stuffed with a meat, vegetable or cheese filling
Rigatoni	Large grooved tubes
Spaghetti	Spaghetti can still be sub-divided into capellini, fusilli, spaghettini, spirale and vermicelli.
Tagliatelle	Ribbon pasta about a quarter of an inch wide
Tortellini	Little twists of pasta with a rich stuffing and delicate sauces
Tortelloni	Large coils of stuffed pasta

11.3 Guide to the menu

Zuppe e Antipasti	*Soups and Starters*
Gamberetti	Shrimps
Granchio	Crabs
Melone con fichi	Melon with figs
Melone con prosciutto	Melon with ham
Misto or frutti di mare	Mixed seafood
Panada	Broth
Zuppa di pesce	Fish soup
Zuppa di fagioli	Bean soup

Risotti e Pasta	*Rice and Pasta dishes*
Asparagi	Risotto with asparagus
Nere de seppie	Risotto with cuttlefish in its ink
Primavera	Risotto with diced fresh vegetables
Bigoli	Dark coloured pasta
Pasta e fagioli	Pasta with white bean soup
Risi e Anguilla	Rice and eel
Risi e bisi	Rice and peas

Pesce e Crostacei	*Fish and shellfish*
Anguilla	Eel
Aringa	Herring
Baccala	Cod
Branzino	Sea bass
Calamari	Squid
Cozze	Mussels
Frutta di mare	Seafood
Gamberetti	Prawns
Granchi	Shrimps
Nasello	Haddock
Ostriche	Oysters
Pesce spada	Swordfish
Salmone	Salmon
Sgombro	Mackerel
Sogliola	Plaice
Sogliola Finta	Sole
Tonno	Tuna
Triglia	Red Mullet
Trota	Trout

Carne	*Meat*
Agnello	Lamb
Anatra/anitra	Duck
Bistecca	Steak
Bistecca de Filetto	Fillet steak
Braciola	Cutlet, chop
Bue	Beef
Coniglio	Rabbit
Coscia	Leg
Cotoletta/Costata	Cutlet/chop
Fagiono	Pheasant
Fegato	Liver

Maiale	Pork
Manzo	Beef
Montone	Mutton
Pollo	Chicken
Prosciutto	Ham
Ragout	Stew
Rognoni	Kidneys
Rosbif	Roast beef
Salsicce	Sausage
Salsicce alla Griglia	Grilled sausage
Selvaggina	Venison
Tacchino	Turkey
Tournedo	Rump steak
Vitello	Veal

Verdura	*Vegetables*
Aglio	Garlic
Barbabietola/Bietola	Beetroot
Broccoli	Broccoli
Carciofi	Artichokes
Carote	Carrots
Cavolfiore	Cauliflower
Cetriolo	Cucumber
Cipolle	Onions
Fagioli	Beans
Funghi	Mushrooms
Insalata	Salad
Lattuga	Lettuce
Melanzana	Aubergines
Patate	Potatoes
Peperoni	Peppers
Piselli	Peas
Pomodoro	Tomato
Spinaci	Spinach

Dolci	*Desserts*
Baicoli	Venetian cookies
Bussolai	Biscuits from Burano
Gelato	Ice cream
Tirami su	Rich dessert in coffee and liqueur, covered in cream
Zuppa inglese	Trifle
Zabaglione	Dessert made with egg yolks and Marsala

Frutta	*Fruit*
Albicocca	Apricot
Ananas	Pineapple
Anguria	Water melon
Arancia	Orange
Cillege	Cherries
Fragole	Strawberries
Frutta fresca	Fresh fruit
Lamponi	Raspberries
Mela	Apple
Pera	Pear
Pesca	Peach
Pompelino	Grapefruit
Prugna	Plum

Bibite	*Drinks*
Acqua Minerale	Mineral water
Birra	Beer
Caffè	Black coffee
Cappuccino	White coffee
Latte	Milk
Tè	Tea
Vino – rosso, bianco	Wine – red, white
dolce, secco, spumante	– sweet, dry, sparkling

Miscellaneous

Burro	Butter
Formaggio	Cheese
Frittata	Omelette
Gnocchi	Dumplings
Minestra	Soup
Pane	Bread
Salsa	Sauce
Uova	Eggs

Cooking terms

Affogate	Poached
Arrosto	Roast
Crudo	Raw
Cotto	Cooked
Fritto	Fried
Strapazzate	Scrambled
Stufato	Stewed

11.4 Typical Venetian specialities

Fegato alla Veneziana – Calf's liver thinly sliced and cooked in butter with onions

Baccalà alla Vicentina – Salt cod simmered in milk

Polenta – The traditional North Italian pudding of boiled maize flour which can be accompanied by a variety of sauces, and served with game, mushrooms, sausages etc

Risi e bisi – risotto with peas

Regional wines: medium dry white Soave; the full-bodied dry red Valpolicella and the Bardolino; dry white Tocai; and the bubbly Prosecco de Conegliano, which is dry white or rosé.

11.5 Restaurant suggestions

Price guideline
Prices in the listed restaurants may be subject to change; and obviously everyone orders differently. But here's the price grading system:

£	=	under £15, often much less
££	=	£20-£30
£££	=	£30+

Restaurants for special occasions

Daniele's, Riva degli Schiavoni   Tel: 5226480
Very special restaurant with outside terrace. Great Mediterranean gourmet specialities. A wonderful restaurant with an enchanting panorama of the Lagoon. Booking essential.   £££

Antica Besseta,   Tel: 721687
Salizzada del Zusto, Giacomo dell'Orio
Home cooking and very few tourists. Reservations essential.   £££

Café Orientale, Rio Marin, S. Polo 2426   £££
Elegant and sophisticated, with canal terrace. Reservations advisable.   Tel: 719804

La Corte Sconta, Calle Pestrin Castello £££
'Hidden Courtyard', famous for fish dishes and Jewish pastries. Tel: 5227024

Do Forni, Calle Specchier, 468 San Marco £££
Expensive, but a jet-set favourite. The interior is a reconstruction of an Orient Express carriage. Closed Thursdays. Tel: 5237729

Alla Borsa, San Moise Tel: 5238819
Offers a good menu. £££

Eating at reasonable prices – Trattorie

Alla Madonna Tel: 5223824
Calle della Madonna, near Rialto
Extremely busy fish restaurant. ££

Burchielle, Santa Croce 393 Tel: 5231342
A simple trattoria, very popular with the local Venetians. ££

Taverna San Trovaso Tel: 5203703
Rio San Trovase, Dorsoduro
Popular with locals. Everything from pizzas to 4-course meals. ££

Povoledo, Lista di Spagna Tel: 716038
Varied menu, and a good tourist menu. Outside terrace on Grand Canal. ££

Da Mario alla Fava, Calle dei Stagne
Reputable restaurant with excellent service. Varied menu, popular with locals. £££

Zanze, Santa Croce 231 Tel: 5223555
Small, stylish, typically Venetian – a lovely restaurant off the beaten track. Serves excellent fresh fish. Offers a special-price menu. ££

Ristorante da Raffaele Tel: 5232317
S. Marco Ponte delle Ostreghe
Typical Venetian cuisine. Seating by the Canal. ££

Vino Vino, Ponte delle Veste (near Fenice Theatre)
Wine bar, open late. Large selection of top quality wine and snacks. Typical Venetian dishes also served. ££

Pizzerias

There are lots of these scattered around Venice, with the usual wide selection of toppings.

DINING OUT

Da Sandro   Tel: 5234894
Campiello Meloni, S. Polo
Small but characteristic, with excellent pizzas.   £

Alle Oche, S. Crose Campo San Giacomo Dall
'Orio (near Camposa Giacomo)   Tel: 5241161
The best pizzas in Venice. Especially popular with
young people.   £

All' Capon, Campo Santa Margarita
Extremely good pizzas.   £

All Sportivo, Campo Santa Margarita   £

Cafés & bars

Harry's Bar, St. Mark's Square
Worth dropping in for an aperitif, as you can even
pay for your drink by American Express! Let the
barman recommend which speciality is in season.

Café Florian, St Mark's Square
Opened in 1720, this is reputed to have been the
first coffee house in Europe. In the summer
months, an orchestra plays. The prices match the
fame, and a cup of coffee will cost a fortune. However, it is worth the treat, for the view alone.

Quadri
Located on the other side of the square from the
Café Florian, almost as old and just as famous.

Harry's Dolci
773 di Sant' Eufemia (on the Guidecca)
For the sweet-toothed, it is sheer luxury. It's also
possible to eat lunch or dinner, followed by the
cakes (dolci). They even serve champagne from the
pump.

Da Leoni, Hotel Londra, Riva degli Schiavoni
Upmarket cocktail bar with piano music. Set in a
superb location, overlooking the lagoon.

Chapter Twelve

Looking at art

12.1 Venice as art patron

Unlike Rome and Florence with their much longer history, the Venetians had no significant buildings or artistic heritage until they became rich and powerful traders about 1,000 years ago.

Their trading links with the Eastern Mediterranean and Middle East exposed them strongly to the art and architecture of Byzantium. With their later share of Crusader loot from Constantinople, the early architects of Venice displayed a cultural mix of Gothic and Byzantine with a touch of Islam. Thanks to a succession of rebuildings and additions, St Mark's Basilica and the Doge's Palace represent an incredible mixture and fusion of styles.

When the merchants of Venice became so wealthy, and the city could so readily afford great splendour in its churches and public buildings, the finest painters, sculptors, craftsmen and architects of Italy settled here and established flourishing studios and workshops.

Masters of the Venetian School

The word 'school' has nothing to do with teaching! It is applied to the artists of different nations, and of groups of painters within one nation. Italian School – a label mainly applied to the Renaissance artists – is sub-divided into regional schools which each had its individual character, reflecting the local environment and taste of the time. Art experts distinguish between about twenty schools of Italian painting, of which Florence, Venice and Siena are among the most important.

LOOKING AT ART

Techniques

Obviously there was an overlap of styles and techniques, especially when artists moved from the patronage of one city to another. But part of the pleasure of looking at Italian paintings comes from recognising this variety between the regional schools.

As the Church was the single most important patron, religious art predominated. Until the late 13th century, Italian art was influenced mainly by Byzantine techniques of working with mosaic. Pictures depicted rather stiff and gloomy characters in the story of Jesus against a formal gold background.

Fresco painting flourished, to reach its perfection during the early 16th century in the hands of Raphael and Michelangelo. Oil painting – invented about 1500 – then took over in popularity.

The great names of the Venetian School were Bellini, Crivelli, Giorgione, Titian, Palma, Carpaccio, Tintoretto, Veronese, Moroni, Guardi, Zuccarelli and Tiepolo.

Their work is characterised by a sensuous quality which focussed on bodily beauty more than spirituality. Pictures reflect the luxury of 15th-century Church and State, when material prosperity was at its height.

In contrast, the Florentines preferred a soft tenderness in their paintings, compared with the raw vigour of the Venetians. In the use of colour, the Florentine School inclined towards a cooler approach – rose and purple blue compared with the Venetian leaning towards opulent orange.

12.2 Thousand years of Italian art

Romanesque (11th-12th centuries)

During the early Middle Ages – before Venice came into existence – pagan Roman basilicas were converted into churches. New church building followed the basic theme of a long hall with two aisles and a semi-circular apse at the far end.

During the 11th century, there was a great wave of church building in all Italian cities. The intense activity led to much innovation in architectural techniques and styles, while artists began to create highly individual works of pictorial and sculptural decoration.

The word 'Romanesque' originally stood for architecture 'in the Roman style', especially in the use of the rounded arch and barrel vaulting. Churches kept mostly to the earlier Christian basilica form with a three-aisled nave, a transept and a semi-circular apse roofed by a half-dome.

Most of the Italian churches of the period stayed with the tradition of wooden ceilings or open rafters. Sculpture was confined mainly to reliefs. The most important Italian centre for sculpture at this time was the Lombardy region focussed on Milan.

Interior church decoration was almost entirely in the form of frescoes, following traditions that were well established from Roman and early Christian times.

Gothic (12th-14th centuries)

A new outlook came through the teachings of St Francis of Assisi (1182-1226) who preached a more gentle and lovable religion in contrast to the former stern austerity.

Painters broke loose from the formal conventions of the Byzantine School, with Giotto leading the way to a fresh and life-like style.

In place of the austere Byzantine backgrounds, biblical stories were set in contemporary dress amid local scenery with familiar hills and countryside. Easel painting came into more general use around this time, permitting a more subtle expression of deep emotions.

Meanwhile, Italian gothic monuments provided large wall and ceiling areas for mural decoration. During this period, the principal technique of fresco painting was based on wet plaster – just enough being applied to a working surface that could be finished in a single day's session.

Painters had to work fast, before the plaster dried out. Compositions were mapped out in red chalk. Filling in the details was a team effort, with the master craftsman directing the operation.

Renaissance (15th-16th centuries)

The Renaissance or cultural 'rebirth' of the 15th and 16th centuries marked the end of the Middle Ages, with a revolution in thought that rediscovered the creative heritage of classical Greek and Roman philosophy, literature and science. The revived interest in the classical world opened up new art themes based on Greek and Roman history and mythology. Artists themselves emerged as imaginative creators rather than as mere craftsmen. In the artistic and cultural history of Western Europe, the Renaissance had the deepest possible influence.

Although Giotto was an isolated forerunner, Early Renaissance developed from a generation of artists who worked in Florence at the start of the 15th century. The trend-setters were Donatello for sculpture, Brunelleschi for architecture and Masaccio for painting – later followed in mid-century by Botticelli in Florence and Giovanni Bellini in Venice. Although Florence remained the centre of innovation throughout the 15th century, other schools followed similar lines, especially in Milan, Venice, Padua and Naples.

In a supremely productive period, about 1495-1520, a few artists of great genius – Leonardo da Vinci, Michelangelo, Bramante, Raphael and Titian – brought a High Renaissance style to perfection. Five centuries later, their works are part of the heritage of modern man.

Late Renaissance and Mannerism (16th-17th centuries)

The sack of Rome in 1527 by the German and Spanish troops of Holy Roman Emperor Charles V marked· the temporary end of Papal patronage. Many leading artists moved to other centres in Italy, Spain and France. Meanwhile, in this Late Renaissance period, a new style called Mannerism had evolved, characterised by highly refined grace and elegance.

This was the age of Palladio and Caravaggio, Cellini, Tintoretto and Veronese, whose prolific works are found throughout North and Central Italy, with Venice richly endowed.

Baroque (17th-18th centuries)

By the end of the 16th century, Mannerism had run its course, to be superseded by the highly ornate Baroque style. Caravaggio set the trend in painting, Bernini in sculpture and Borromini in architecture. Baroque was introduced to northern Europe mainly through Rubens, who had studied in Italy during the formative period of 1600-1608. But the main centre of Baroque for most of the 17th century was Rome.

The spectacular style became highly popular throughout the Catholic world, and also among monarchs and other wealthy secular patrons. The style survived into the 18th century, to be replaced in turn by Rococo. Among the leading Venetian artists of the period were Canaletto, Guardi and Tiepolo. With their passing, the greatest days of Italian painting came to an end.

Chapter Thirteen
Who's who in art

13.1 The principal Venetian artists

Here are some brief notes on a few of the leading artists whose work can be seen in Venice, or who influenced the development of Italian art.

Bassano – An entire family of painters (originally from Bassano, hence the name!) who were active in Venice from early 16th to early 17th century. The most gifted member of the family was Jacopo (1517-1592) who adopted the Florentine Mannerist style from the 1540's.

He was skilled in portrayal of animals and rustic figures, and the adoption of dramatic light and shadow effects.

Bellini – A family of 15th-century Renaissance artists: Jacopo (1400-1470) and his two sons, Gentile (1429-1507) and Giovanni (1430-1516). The father's paintings were in Venetian Gothic style, and his sons served their apprenticeship in the Venice studio.

The most talented member of the family was Giovanni, who was appointed as the painter to the Venetian Republic in 1483.

In that capacity he received numerous commissions for official portraits and for a number of large altarpieces on which he shared the work with his brother Gentile.

He was a pioneer in the use of oils in preference to tempera (powdered pigments with egg yolk and water). Among his pupils were Giorgione and Titian.

Canaletto – 1697-1768, was a Venetian master of cityscapes, with every detail painted with great topographical accuracy. A master of perspective, he also captured the atmosphere of his native city. Apart from two lengthy periods in England from 1746 to 1755, and a brief stay in Rome, his entire life was dedicated to Venice. Together with his contemporary Guardi, Canaletto is one of the great recorders of 18th-century Venice.

Canova – 1757-1822, is rated by some authorities as the greatest sculptor after Michelangelo. He was a leading exponent of Neoclassicism, reviving the basic themes and styles of the ancient Romans. Born near Venice, he received his early training there, graduating to his own studio at the age of 17. His early maturity is demonstrated by the *Daedelus and Icarus*, produced in 1778 and now in the Correr Museum. In 1779 he moved to Rome. His social prestige gave him innumerable commissions from aristocratic patrons in Rome, Venice and London. Although a bachelor of abstemious habits, he produced extremely sensuous work.

Carpaccio – 1465-1526. A major Renaissance painter, Vittore Carpaccio was born in Venice of an old Venetian family. His finest work was produced in a 30-year period from 1490: large canvases that depicted many sides of Venetian contemporary life in traditional and legendary themes. His principal works were commissioned by the confraternities of Venice. In the Accademia are nine scenes of *The Legend of St Ursula*. Another nine large canvases depicting the lives of Saints George, Trifone and Jerome, are displayed in the Scuola di San Giorgio degli Schiavoni. Other masterpieces are hung in the Ca' d'Oro and the Correr galleries.

Giorgione – 1477-1510. As a talented Venetian poet, musician and painter, Giorgione played a key role in the early 16th-century shift to High Renaissance style.

In his brief career (cut short by the Plague), he initially worked as a pupil of the Bellini brothers, but then began to absorb some of the techniques of Leonardo da Vinci. Several paintings attributed to Giorgione were completed by his contemporary, Titian, who was greatly influenced by Giorgione's innovations, which Titian developed during his long life.

Guardi – 1712-1793. A self-taught painter of the Venetian scene, Guardi was influenced by Canaletto but adopted a totally different style. His delicate touch evoked the atmosphere of the city with brilliant use of colour and sweeping brush-strokes.

Lorenzo Lotto – 1480-1556. A Venetian painter, Lotto worked in many Italian cities, but was particularly exposed to the High Renaissance style of Florence and Rome. He worked for several years with other artists, decorating the apartments of Pope Julius II – a task which was later completed by Raphael. Returning to Venice with that rich experience, he is specially admired for his Venetian portraits which capture the image of the 16th century.

Palladio – 1508-1580. One of the greatest architects of the High Renaissance, Andrea Palladio worked mainly in Venice, Vicenza and in Veneto province. Trained as a stone-carver, he spent years in studying classical art and architecture during numerous field visits to Rome. His 'Four Books of Architecture' took 20 years to prepare and were finally published in 1570.

His published works, and the villas and churches he built, influenced architects throughout Europe in the Palladian style, through numerous editions and translations. In Venice his two greatest monuments are the Church of San Giorgio Maggiore (1565) and the Redentore (1576).

Palma Vecchio – 1480-1528. Jacopo Palma was a pupil in Giovanni Bellini's studio, and was also greatly influenced by Giorgione and Titian. His works – mainly of blonde and buxom female saints – are represented in the Accademia and in the church of Santa Maria Formosa.

Palma Giovane – 1544-1628. A grand-nephew of Palma 'the Elder' (see above), the 'young' Palma followed the styles of Bassano and Tintoretto. His numerous works are located in several Venetian churches, the Doge's Palace and in the Accademia.

Sansovino – 1486-1570. Of Florentine origin, the sculptor and architect Jacopo Sansovino moved in 1505 to Rome, where he absorbed a classical style through his initial work of renovating ancient Roman statues.

From 1527 he resettled in Venice, where his experience in Rome and Florence was utilised in the High Renaissance design of several major buildings of the historic centre, including the Mint, the Library, and the Palazzo Corner della Ca' Grande.

The Ca' Grande set the style for many of the other palaces and mansions which line the Grand Canal. His most noticeable sculptures are the huge figures of Mars and Neptune at the staircase entrance to the Doge's Palace.

Tiepolo – 1696-1769. A highly prolific painter in the High Renaissance style, Giambattista Tiepolo had a dazzling technique and style which never lacked patrons wherever he worked in Venice, northern Italy, Germany and Spain.

Tiepolo's death in 1769 effectively marked the end of the greatest era of Italian painting, though his two sons – Gian Domenico and Lorenzo – continued to work in the same tradition.

Tintoretto – 1518-1594 – was a Venetian painter on the grand scale, producing large and numerous works for the Doge's Palace and a cycle of paintings for the Scuola of the Confraternity of San Rocco.

His themes ranged from historic battle scenes to religious and mythological subjects. Two sons and a daughter were part of the production line of pupils and assistants.

Tintoretto's work was Mannerist in style, combining the colour techniques of Titian with the drawing of Michelangelo.

Titian – 1488-1576. During his long and productive life, Titian created hundreds of masterly portraits and religious and mythological paintings. He studied in Venice under the brothers Gentile and Giovanni Bellini, but the greatest influence came from Giorgione, with whom he was closely associated. Titian adopted many of Giorgione's innovations in colour and brush techniques, and in his poetic interpretation of figures and landscape. Titian ranks as the greatest Renaissance painter of Venice, and a major contributor to the history of European art.

Veronese – 1528-1588. Trained in Verona (hence his name) Paolo Veronese spent most of his working life in Venice, where he ranked alongside the other great 16th-century Renaissance painters, Titian and Tintoretto.

At the age of 25 he leapt to fame with his ceiling panels in the Doge's Palace. His theatrical style even with religious works put him in trouble with the Inquisition when he painted a Last Supper which was crowded with exotic characters. He renamed the picture *Feast in the House of the Levi*, which is now in the Accademia.

Zuccarelli – 1702-1788. A Venetian baroque landscape painter, Francesco Zuccarelli found many wealthy English patrons among the aristocratic visitors to 18th-century Venice. He resided in London for a ten-year period from 1752; and another six years from 1765.

During that time he became a founder member of the Royal Academy. He specialised in elegant landscapes with classic ruins. Several paintings are in the Accademia.

13.2 Who's who among the gods

From the Renaissance onwards, artists turned more frequently to subjects based on classical Roman mythology, which often had been adapted from the pantheon of the Greeks. Here's a short list of the more popular characters.

Apollo – or Phoebus, the sun god; the god of prophesy, music, song and the arts. Protector of flocks and herds.

Bacchus – Dionysos – god of vegetation, and the fruits of the trees, especially wine.

Cupid – the Greek Eros – the lovers' favourite.

Diana – otherwise known as Artemis – deity of the chase; goddess of the moon, protectress of the young. Sister of Apollo.

Fortuna – the Greek Tyche – personifying fortune, usually depicted holding a rudder, or with a globe or cornucopia.

Juno – Hera among the Greeks – the good wife of Jupiter.

Jupiter – Zeus – greatest of the Olympian Gods; father of both gods and men.

Mars – father of the twin founders of Rome, he was a Roman favourite with several temples to his name.

Medusa – one of the three Gorgon sisters – lost her head to Perseus, blood everywhere.

Mercury – Hermes – messenger of the gods, who usually wore a travelling hat, golden sandals, and a purse. Mercury was patron of merchants, thieves, artists, orators and travellers.

Minerva – based on the Greek Athena, goddess of war and wisdom; patroness of agriculture, industry and the arts.

Nemesis – the fatal divinity, measuring out happiness and unhappiness.

Neptune – Poseidon – god of the sea, and responsible for earthquakes.

Venus – otherwise known as Aphrodite – goddess of love and beauty; the Marilyn Monroe of classical times. Sometimes appears with a sea-horse or dolphin. Julius Caesar claimed her as an ancestor.

Chapter Fourteen

Travel hints

14.1 Money and Banking

The Italian unit of currency is the lira (plural lire).

Coins	Notes
50 lire	1,000 lire
100 lire	2,000 lire
200 lire	5,000 lire
500 lire	10,000 lire
	50,000 lire
	100,000 lire

The symbol used for marking prices is either a letter 'L', or similar to the pound sterling sign – £.

Unless you're very fast at mental arithmetic, Italian lire are confusing for the first day or two, unless it's a handy equivalent such as 2,500 lire to the pound. Suggestion: before departure, check the current exchange rate, and list out some conversions on a postcard, as a handy crib.

There is often a shortage of small change, and telephone tokens (worth 200 lire), sweets or stamps may be used to make up the deficiency.

Changing Money
Take a starter kit of a bundle of lire, to tide you over the first day or two in Italy, especially if you arrive at weekends.

You can change money and cheques at the arrival airport or railway terminus. Banks are normally open 8.30 a.m. till 1.20 p.m., and for a variable hour in the afternoon, Monday till Friday, closed weekends.

Commission charges

Rates vary slightly from bank to bank, so it's worth comparing their display panels. A flat commission charge of up to 3000 lire on Traveller Cheques makes it uneconomic to change little and often. Some Exchange Bureaux keep longer hours, and take a bigger slice of your money. Larger hotels can also oblige, but give even lower rates.

Remember to take your passport when changing money.

Personal Cheques & Eurocheques

Backed by the appropriate banker's card, Eurocheques are among the simplest and most acceptable means of payment. These must be specially ordered from your bank, but are well worth it, as you can then write cheques in the local currency. They can also be used in UK.

The Eurocheque card allows you to cash up to £120 on each cheque, and is valid for making payments to shops, hotels and restaurants that display the 'ec' sign. Many places also accept normal cheques up to £50 if backed by a banker's card.

Credit Cards

Access, Visa, American Express and Diners Club are widely accepted at shops and restaurants. At some banks you can withdraw cash, but it's often inconvenient. Don't over-rely on credit cards for getting cash, though automatic cash machines are becoming more prevalent.

Banks & Exchange Bureaux

Opening hours for banks in Venice are Mon-Fri 8.30-13.30 and 14.45-15.45 hrs. There's wide choice in the city centre, but here's a short list.

Credito Italiano
Riva del Carbon, San Salvador 5058
San Marco, Bocca di Piazza Ascensione

Cassa Di Risparmio Di Venezia
Centro Storico, Campo Manin
Piazzale Roma, Santa Croce 458

Banco San Marco, Santa Lucia Station F.S. 122

TRAVEL HINTS

Exchange Bureau open late

Ferrovia, Railway Station – Open daily 8-13 and 15-20 hrs.

Various other exchange bureaux are scattered around the city, especially in the St Mark's Square area. They are usually closed Saturday afternoon and Sundays.

Reconverting cash

In general, convert any surplus lire back into ster-ling or dollars at the departure airport. Avoid taking 50,000 and 100,000 lire notes back into the UK, as banks may refuse to change them and certainly will give a lower rate.

14.2 Security

Pickpockets

Just like in any other European country, Italy's main cities have their quota of hardworking pick-pockets who specialise in the tourist traffic. Their guess is that holidaymaker handbags or wallets will contain an above-average supply of currency, travel-ler cheques and credit cards. The light-fingered gentry are not necessarily bent Italians. International teams are also at work during the season, often looking just like other tourists.

Be particularly careful in crowded places, espe-cially if travelling by vaporetti where your attention is focussed on the Grand Canal scenery. Thieves often work in pairs, taking advantage of crowds to jostle or distract their victims while stealing a purse or wallet. There's no need to go overboard with suspicion of all strangers. But it's sensible not to make things easy for crooks.

Never carry a wallet in your hip pocket. Keep handbags fastened and held securely. In a café or restaurant, don't hang camera or handbag over the back of your chair.

Minimise any potential loss by leaving the bulk of your valuables in the safety deposits available to hotel guests. Keep a separate record of traveller cheque numbers, and also of credit-card details of where to notify in case of loss. It also helps to have a photo-copy of your passport details.

Loss report

If you have anything stolen, report the theft to the nearest police station and obtain an official declaration of theft, required for insurance reclaim. If you're on a package tour with insurance cover, contact the travel-agency representative for advice on making a 'Loss Report' to send with your claim form.

If your passport has gone missing, once you have the police report you should go to the British Consulate at Dorsoduro 1051 (on Grand Canal, by Accademia Bridge – Tel: 52 27207), taking two passport size photographs. The Consulate will issue a temporary passport to get you home.

Female harrassment

Of course, it does exist. Best advice is to ignore the persistent overtures, until the idiots get tired of the game and try elsewhere. Otherwise, say "NO!" in loud English. It means the same in Italian. You could also respond in basic Anglo-Saxon, which would be equally well understood.

14.3 Postal and phone services

Post Offices (Ufficio Postale) handle telegrams, mail and money transfers, and some have public telephones. Opening hours are generally Mon-Sat 8.15-14.00 hours. The system gets low marks for efficiency. Air mail seems to travel by slow pigeon, and you'll easily race postcards home.

Main Post Office – Poste Centrali Rialto, Fondaco dei Tedeschi. The telegram office is open 24 hours a day.

Branch Offices – Lista di Spagna 233; and Campo San Stefano 2801.

Stamps are also sold at tobacconists' (tabaccheria) with a 'T' sign above the door. They're a lot more helpful if you buy some postcards at the same time. Likewise, some hotel desks carry a stamp supply. Stamps are 'francobolli' in Italian.

Post boxes are red, and non-local mail should be posted in the slot marked 'altre destinazioni'.

Phoning home

Making long distance and international calls from hotels is an expensive luxury. Instead, go to the nearest office of TELECOM. There's a line of cabins, and a queue. When your turn comes, the counter clerk will tell you which booth number to use.

● Dial 00 for International Exchange, and wait for a tone change.

● Dial 44 (the international code for UK) plus the appropriate STD town dialling code, minus the first zero; then the local number. Thus, to call Barnsley (code 01226) 12345, dial 0044 1226 12345. Other country codes are: USA and Canada 1; Australia 61; New Zealand 64; Eire 353.

● Afterwards, you return to the desk to pay for the telephone call at the regular cost with no mark-ups. Calls are cheaper after 11 p.m. or before 8 a.m., and throughout the weekend from 14.30 hrs on Saturday.

Telephone offices – The main Telecom office is near Rialto Bridge in the Campo San Bartolomeo. Open daily 8.30 a.m. till midnight.

At the Railway Station there's another office, open daily 8-20 hours.

Marco Polo Airport has an S.I.P. office in the main departure hall.

Phone cards called *scheda*, costing 5,000 or 10,000 lire at Telecom offices and tobacconists, are the best way of making international phone calls. When you buy a new card, tear off the corner where it says *stracciare* or *strappare* – otherwise the card will not completely enter the slot. The residual value shows on the screen. Long distance calls can be made from telephone boxes with a yellow disc and the word 'teleselezione' or 'interurbana'.

Coin boxes: For local calls, you'll need two 100-lire coins or one 200-lire coin for the modern call box; or occasionally a *gettone* (token) which costs 200 lire at a bar. Lift receiver, insert the coins or token and dial. 'Guasto' means broken or out of order.

Reverse charge calls to UK or North America can be placed by inserting your basic 200 lire, and dialling 172 followed by the national code. You then negotiate your reverse-charge number with the operator in the home country. If you come equipped with a British Telecom chargecard – or AT&T for North America – the cost can be charged to your home number.

To call Venice from other countries, the international code is 39-41. Thus, from Britain, dial 00-39-41 followed by the local number in Venice. From North America, dial 011-39-41 etc.

14.4 Medical

As part of EEC reciprocal health arrangements, UK visitors can get all medical services that are available to Italians. Before departure from Britain, ask your local Department of Health and Social Security (DHSS) office for the "Medical Costs Abroad" leaflet no. SA30. Fill out the form CM1 and send it to the DHSS, who will supply form E111 to take with you. It's probably not worth the effort for minor ailments, but would be most useful if anything major happened.

Should you require a doctor, contact your hotel concierge and ask him to call one.

If you have holiday or medical insurance, get receipts both from the doctor and the chemist, so as to make any necessary reclaim. If you're on a package tour, and sizeable funds are needed to cover medical expenses, contact your travel-agency rep for advice.

If mosquitoes normally have you for supper, bring some repellent. Biting insects are most active in July and August. To ensure peaceful sleep, you can outwit night-flying insects by keeping bedroom windows closed and air conditioning switched on. It's also worth packing an electrically-operated mosquito kit, which can be remarkably effective.

A combination of hot weather, iced drinks and different food can cause tummy problems. If the bug hits, doctors advise drinking plenty of fruit juice – such as lemon or orange – or bottled water with a twitch of sugar and salt (to counter dehydration). Continue eating normally. Among the pharmaceuticals, Lomotil, Imodium and Arrêt are usually effective, and one of those may be worth packing. Local doctors can provide stronger preparations if necessary.

You have to be desperate, to use the facilities in some of the canal-side cafés which you may wish to visit in a hurry. Sometimes the gap between utter misery and fulfillment is measured by a few sheets of toilet paper. Always carry supplies in your hold-all, in case of emergencies.

Chemists are open only during normal shop hours, but a window sign indicates the nearest night or Sunday-opening chemist ('farmacia').

14.5 What to wear and pack

Casual dress is OK for tourist Venice, though you may prefer something more formal for any up-market evening dining or a visit to the Casino. Most likely you'll be on your feet most of the day, so forget about high heels. Comfortable flat footwear is much better.

To enter St Mark's and other Venetian churches you should be soberly dressed: no shorts; no above-the-knee skirts; no sleeveless dresses (though women can get by with a scarf draped over shoulders). Otherwise you could be politely turned away.

Pack binoculars or opera glasses for better viewing of paintings, mosaics and the details of palaces along the Grand Canal.

If you want to use any electric gadgets, pack a plug adaptor. Venice is on 220 volts, but uses the Continental-type 2-pin plug.

Don't worry if your cosmetic, pharmaceutical or film supplies run out. All the major brands are readily available in Venice. However, take far more camera film than ever you'd carry to any other European destination. The number of photo subjects is unbelievable. Why waste precious time buying film in Venice at higher prices than back home?

In the expectation of buying some stylish Italian clothing, many visitors travel out light in their luggage to leave room for the loot.

14.6 Home news

The English-language newspapers which arrive first in Venice are *The Guardian*, *Financial Times*, *International Herald Tribune* and *The Wall Street Journal* – all printed on the Continent. Other London newspapers and magazines normally arrive by afternoon, and cost about double the UK price.

Most of the larger hotels are now equipped to receive satellite TV, and can offer 24-hour choice of CNN, Sky News and similar programmes.

If your holiday would be ruined without important home news like up-to-date Test Match scores, it's worth packing a short-wave radio, to catch the regular on-the-hour news bulletins of the BBC World Service. The best wave-lengths for Venice are:

Early morning – 9410 on 31-meter band; 6195 on 49m band; 3955 on 75m band.
Daytime – 12095 on 25-meter band; 15070 on 19m band; 9750 on 31m band.
Evening – 9410 on 31m band; 6195 on 49m band; 7325 on 41m band.

Reception varies greatly according to time and location. Reception can be greatly improved with an external aerial. A length of wire dangling over your balcony can make all the difference.

Medium or Long Wave cannot be relied upon, but you could always try your luck on 648 Medium Wave or 198 Long Wave.

Chapter Fifteen

Further reference

15.1 Public holidays

1 January	New Year's Day
6 January	Epiphany
25 April	Liberation Day, 1945
Easter Monday	
1 May	May Day
15 August	Assumption
1 November	All Saints
8 December	Immaculate Conception
25 December	Christmas Day
26 December	St Stephen's Day

Venetians also take November 21 as a holiday for Festa della Salute, commemorating the end of a plague in 1631.

Be prepared for a three-day closure of banking and other services when any of these holidays makes a bridge with the weekend.

15.2 Whom to contact

Emergency
Police – Fire Brigade – Ambulance –   Dial 113

Police – Passport and Foreigners Dept
Castello 5053   Tel: 703222
If money or passport is stolen, report to this office and obtain a 'declaration of theft' – essential for any insurance claim. There is a local police station in each section of the city.

First Aid – Piazza San Marco   Tel: 5286346
Open Mon-Sat 8-20 hrs.

Hospital – Casualty Departments   Tel: 761750
Ospedale al Mare (Lungomare d'Annunzio / Lido)
i Civili Rivuti di Venezia   Tel: 705622
Campo Santi Giovanni e Paulo

Pharmaceutical Chemists
Open: Mon-Fri 9-12.30 & 15.30-19.15 hrs.
Sat 9-12.45 hrs.
There is a chemist in each district. Name and ad-
dress of the night-chemist is always displayed on
the door. Alternatively ring: 192.

Lost property
For losses on public transport:
If lost on a vaporetto apply to the office of "Oggetti
rinvenuti" at the A.C.T.V. (stop number 9, San
Angelo); or A.C.N.I.L. (City Public Transport).
For losses elsewhere: Riva del Carbon, Pallazo
Farsetti (City Hall), Campo San Luca.

Consulates
*Most European countries maintain a consulate in
Venice; otherwise the nearest will most likely be
located in Milan.*
British Consulate, Dorsoduro 1051   Tel: 5227207
On the Grand Canal, by Accademia Bridge
US Consulate   Tel: (02)-290351
Largo Donegani 1, Milan
Australian Consulate   Tel: (02)-6598727
Via Turati 40, Milan
Canadian Consulate   Tel: (02)-6697451
Via Vittor Pisani 19, Milan

Venice Tourist Information
Information Offices are located at:
San Marco   5226356
S. Lucia Railway Station   715016
Venice Lido   5265721
Provincial Tourist office, Castello 4421   5298711

REFERENCE

More Information

If you require any more holiday information before you travel, contact the Italian State Tourist Office (ENIT for short):

London – 1 Princes Street, London W1R 8AY. Tel: (0171) 408-1254. Mon-Fri 9-14.30 hrs.
New York – 630 Fifth Avenue, Suite 1565, New York, NY 10111. Tel: (212) 245-4822/4.
Chicago – 500 North Michigan Avenue, Chicago, IL 60611. Tel: (312) 644-0990/1.
Los Angeles – 12400 Wilshire Blvd., Suite 550, Los Angeles, CA 90025. Tel: (310) 820-0098.
Montreal – 1 Place Ville Marie, Suite 1914, Montreal, Quebec. Tel: (514) 866-7667.

In Venice itself, try to acquire or borrow from your hotel a free publication called "Venice – Concierge Information", packed with current timings and prices for museums and galleries, concerts, exhibitions, events, etc.